Practical

Proofreading

Pam Collings

Published by Pam Collings

Copyright © Pam Collings 2021

The National Library of Australia
Cataloguing-in-Publication Data

Collings, Pam
Practical Proofreading

ISBN 978-0-9923002-1-0 (pbk)

A catalogue record for this work is available from the National Library of Australia

The Author of this book accepts all responsibility
for the contents and absolves any other person or
persons involved in its production from any
responsibility or liability where the contents are concerned.

All rights reserved. No part of this publication
may be reproduced, stored in a retrieval system,
or transmitted, in any form, by any means,
electronic, mechanical, photocopying, recording
or otherwise, without prior permission from the author.

Typeset in Bookman Old Style 10pt

Produced by **TB Books**
        P.O. Box 8138
        Seymour South Victoria 3660 Australia
        Email: tbbooks@collings.id.au

Cover Design by Pam Collings

Contents

A Note from the Author 5

How this book works 6

Introduction 7

What is a proofreader? 9

Am I a proofreader? 9

What basic techniques do I need to know? 10

What tools do I need? 10

A Note about the Layout Designer 11

Some Publishing Terminology 12

Now what? 15

How do I replace characters that are wrong? 23

How do I insert missing characters or words? 27

How do I insert or replace punctuation and spaces? 30

How do I insert or replace dashes? 31

How do I insert or replace other special characters? 32

How do I insert a tab at the start of a paragraph? 37

How do I indicate the need for a new paragraph? 38

How do I insert blank lines between text? 39

How do I delete words or characters that are not needed? 47

How do I remove unwanted spaces? 48

How do I delete unwanted blank lines? 49

How do I remove a paragraph? 49

How do I delete a tab at the beginning of a line? 50

What do I do if words or letters are around the wrong way? 67

How do I move text forward to the next page? 68

How do I move text backwards? 68

How do I change lower case characters to capitals? 85

How do I change capital letters to lower case? 85

How do I change ordinary text to Italics? 86

How do I change Italic text to ordinary text? 87

How do I change text to be bold or bold text to ordinary text? 87

How do I indicate text should be underlined? 88

How do I centre text? 89

How do I make sure lines start in the same place? 90

I've made a mistake. How do I fix it? 99

What do I do if I have a question?	99
Some handy techniques	108
Check list	109
Some Handy references	110
Mark-up symbol table	113
Some more practice to keep you going	117
Solutions to Exercises	149
Solutions to Major Exercises	159
One last note	229

A Note from the Author

Many years ago, I formed a writer's group in my local area. At the time I had no idea that it would lead me down the path of becoming a proofreader and editor.

Until one day I was chatting to one of the members of my group and discovered that she worked as a layout designer for a local publisher, well fairly local, anyway. She started to complain about the quality of the work of one of their proofreaders.

A blow between the eyeballs later and I heard myself piping up that I wouldn't mind getting into that sort of thing. How would I go about it?

Well, the rest is history, as they say, whoever 'they' are.

With the prospect of this new career in mind I went in search of courses that might train me for any work that my friend might be able to secure for me. I didn't find very much really that was helpful. I came to realise that most training in proofreading and editing takes place on the job. Of course, that's a bit hard when you are freelancing.

After some extensive research, I discovered a couple of one-day short courses in proofreading run through RMIT in Melbourne. They were informative and gave me the basics I needed to get started but they left a lot to be desired in regards to practise. Two days is just not enough to learn how to spot errors and how to best use the mark-up language in the clearest and most efficient manner.

In the end I had to rely upon the small amount that I did learn and my own common sense. I made mistakes, or maybe not mistakes, but I had to work most things out by trial and error. Sometimes this was very frustrating, and I often wished that I could practise in between real assignments. But I was unable to find anything appropriate.

Gradually my experience grew, and I became more confident with my abilities.

I have spent several years tutoring correspondence courses in proofreading and editing. This has shown me how hard it is to provide enough exercise material within the framework of a course.

And so the idea for a book began to grow. I wanted it to, not only have the basic information, techniques, and tips for being able to be a good proofreader but have heaps of exercise material for the novice proofreader to use as well. The writing of it has been a long process but now here it finally is.

To make things even more interesting, I have deliberately not had this book proofread, so see what errors you might be able to spot. Practise is definitely the best way to learn.

I hope that you find this book useful.

Pam Collings

How this book works

Just a short word to explain how I have put this book and its exercises together.

The first section gives you some general information about being a proofreader. Then we get into the actual nitty gritty of how to proofread.

I have laid out this book as a series of questions – **How do I do such and such?** I hope that this will help you find your way around a bit more easily to find the correct techniques for a given action.

All the examples and exercises are my own original work, so I will apologise up front for the lack of interesting material.

The mini exercises are bigger pieces of writing that I have split up to illustrate each aspect of the proofreading language or techniques, so in the end you have the whole piece of writing, but it is just a bit disjointed.

The mini exercises, like the major exercises, are contained within a yellow block to make them more easily identified.

Most examples are also a small part of a larger piece of writing.

At the end of the book, I have included a possible solution to all of the exercises. I say 'possible' because sometimes there is more than way to mark something up and every proofreader has their own preferences.

I hope you have fun!

Introduction

What is a proofreader?

A proofreader is the last link in the publication process responsible for the quality of a document. The proofreader checks for any layout problems, grammar, punctuation and spelling errors and any other errors that may compromise the look and accuracy of the document. They do not make changes involving judgement such as substituting words, or phrases or restructuring sentences. This is the responsibility of the copy editor.

The proofreader contributes to the publishing process after the document has been laid out and formatted by the layout designer and any changes they find must be returned to the layout designer for implementation.

Am I a proofreader?

A good question to ask. Everyone can be a proofreader, but some people have more of a natural aptitude for it than others.

To be a good proofreader you need to have the following qualities:

- A good eye for detail.
- A good knowledge of grammar and punctuation (although a feel for such things can be good enough. Exact details can always be looked up).
- Good spelling abilities.
- Be able to follow instructions well.
- Be able to be clear and concise when using the proofreading symbols.
- Someone who is somewhat of a perfectionist.

Even if you don't consider that you have all of these qualities, it is still possible to be a good proofreader with constant practise. This book is one way to gain said practise.

What basic techniques do I need to know?

The basic techniques of a proofreader are fairly straight forward. However, they need to be followed closely in order to be able to work with a large number of different professionals. There are conventions and certain rules that make it easier to work towards editors and layout designers and will ensure that you develop a good reputation in the field of proofreading.

Here are the basic rules and conventions:

- Use a red pen for all markings, unless otherwise instructed.

- Place indications in the text that describe what is to be changed.

- Place corresponding explanations in the margin explaining what the change should be.

- Be as clear as possible. Keeping explanations as simple as possible is generally the best.

- Be as neat as possible to ensure the layout designer does not misunderstand what is required.

- Do not change words or phrases. This is the province of the copy editor. The proofreader looks for errors and omissions – only – thus ensuring the quality of a document. However, it is permissible to return the work to the copy editor if you think there is a need for an alteration that borders on their responsibility.

What tools do I need?

To undertake proofreading as a freelancer, here are the basic tools and equipment you need:

- Somewhere quiet to work.

- A desk or table to work at.

- A good ergonomic chair. You will spend hours bent over and you really don't need an uncomfortable chair for this type of work or else you will end up a cripple.

- Some fine red pens that leave a clean mark and do not smudge.

- A ruler or bookmark to use as a guide.

- A good dictionary. The Macquarie Dictionary is the industry standard in Australia, and you should have one of a reasonable size or better still a subscription to their online dictionary which is kept up to date at all times.

- A good grammar reference or access to the Internet where there are numerous websites you can query when necessary. See the back of this book for some recommended references.

- A good bright desk lamp.

- A computer with relevant software. Contact via the Internet is essential, and the Internet is very handy when needing to check something.

- A printer to print off any instructions to keep them handy.
- Access to the Internet.
- An answering machine to ensure you don't miss any enquiries regarding potential work.
- Business cards to hand out whenever anyone shows the slightest bit of interest in what you do.

A Note about the Layout Designer

The layout designer is responsible for formatting the document to make it look the way it needs to once it is printed. Along with a production team (sometimes) the layout designer will decide on such elements as: the look of headings, size of margins, header and footer appearance and contents, font and size of font, any special treatments – tables, diagrams, photos, decorative elements, page numbering – to name a few.

The layout designer (or typesetter, as they used to be called) works extremely quickly and, therefore, any changes directed to them must be clear and beyond interpretation. Knowing a little about the programs the layout designer uses can help to make your marking more appropriate to the needs of the layout designer. The most commonly used programs for layout design are Adobe InDesign and QuarkXpress. Microsoft Publisher has some of the capabilities of these programs but is a much simpler program and not often used by professionals. However, if you cannot gain knowledge in one of the professional packages, Publisher does help to some extent.

Adobe Indesign has a trial version you can download and play with for a limited time. QuarkXpress also has a 30 day free trial. Try downloading these and having a play with them to get the feel of what the layout designer needs to do.

Just briefly, these packages have such things as Master pages, which contain all the elements of pages that have the same layout. A number of master pages can be used in a given document. The programs enable fitting of text so that things like widows and orphans (see definitions) can be eliminated without being noticeably condensed or expanded. Line spacing can be finely tuned as well. They handle complex documents easily and flexibly, such as reference books containing tables, diagrams and photos, needing multiple columns or other intricate and individual layout.

If you're lucky the layout designer, or a responsible editor, will produce a Style Sheet for the project that details all these elements, including specific spelling of words that can be spelt multiple ways. As a proofreader the Style Sheet is extremely handy, possibly essential, in order to make sure there are no layout problems and that every element is uniform within the document.

If at all possible try to obtain a Style Sheet for any projects you work on. If one does not exist, and time allows, put one together from what information you are given and have it checked by your contact.

Some Publishing Terminology

Many industries have their own specific terminology, and the publishing profession is no exception. Here are some you may come across and need to know.

Adjective	An adjective describes something about a noun, e.g. **beautiful** painting, **spectacular** musical.
Adverb	An adverb describes some aspect about a verb, and often ends in 'ly'. e.g. walking **briskly**, nodding **happily**.
Apostrophe	An apostrophe is a punctuation mark used to indicate possessives, or letters omitted from words, known as a contraction. e.g. **Tom's** shoe (possessive singular form – apostrophe before the s), the **Smiths'** house (possessive plural form – apostrophe after the s), **don't** (contraction). They are referred to as single quotes when used to surround speech.
Ascender	The ascender is the part of a character that sticks up above the main part of a character such as the stick on a *b, d, f, k, or l*.
Blurb	The blurb is the description of a book that appears on the back cover or in publicity material. This is often written by one of the publishing team members.
Bold	Bold type is a heavier or darker print, e.g. **this is bold**.
CIP data	CIP is the abbreviation for Cataloguing-in-Publication data and is used to provide a bibliographic record of a publication. It is essential for publications that will be available in a library.
Character	This is any alphabetic, numeric or symbolic mark used in written language.
Centred	This is the alignment of type so it is central within the margins, or space provided. It has equal space on both the left and right sides if centred horizontally, or above and below if centred vertically.
Comma	The comma is the character used to indicate the slightest pause during reading, or separate elements in a list. e.g. ,
Conjunction	Conjunctions are words that join phrases and words together, e.g. **and**, **but**, **or**.
Descender	The descender is the part of a character that falls below the baseline, such as the tail of a *g, j, p, q and y*.
Double quotes	The double quotation mark is used to indicate speech and looks like two apostrophes but is, in fact, one character. Double quotation marks are used in pairs – one at the start of a piece of dialogue and one at the end. Note that they look slightly different for start and end placement. At the start a double quote has the bulge at the bottom and at the end the bulge is at the top. When marking up changes to a double quote mark, you must treat it as one character not two. e.g. "Hi,"
Exclamation mark	The exclamation mark is placed at the end of a sentence to indicate surprise or emphasis of some sort. e.g. Stop!
Caret	This is the name for the mark that proofreaders use to indicate the position where new matter is to be inserted within a body of text.
Crop Marks	These are the lines that appear on artwork or proofs, which indicate where the final printed document will be trimmed.
Ellipsis	This is a three-dot punctuation mark indicating omitted words or stuttering or run off in dialogue. e.g. 'Well, I don't know …'

Endmatter	These are the pages that follow the main body of the text, including appendixes, notes, bibliography and index.
Em dash	This is a dash the length of the letter 'm' in any given font. It sets something apart from the main part of a sentence, e.g. —
En dash	This is a dash the length of the letter 'n' in any given font, which links something to the main part of a sentence, e.g. –
Font	This is the style of type used in the printed document.
Freelance	This is to work independently in your own business.
Full out	This is type set flush to the left and/or right margins. Sometimes called 'justified'.
Full stop	This is one of several punctuation marks that indicate the end of a sentence, e.g. .
Gutter	This is the margin between two facing pages. It also refers to the space between columns on a page.
Half-title page	This page has the main title of the book only.
House Style	This is the publisher's preferred spelling, grammar and format for their publications.
Hyphen	This is a dash that is used to join the parts of a compound word or the parts of a word divided for any reason. It is shorter than an em dash and an en dash, e.g. -
Imprint page	This page contains the name and address of the publisher and printer, copyright information, CIP data, ISBN number and publication details, including cover design credit and statements regarding reproduction of the publication.
Indent	An indent occurs when a line of type is set so that it begins or ends inside the normal margins.
In-house	This is to work as an employee of a company.
ISBN	This stands for International Standard Book Number and is a 10-digit or 13-digit number. (It changed to a 13-digit number on 1 January 2007).
Italic	This is the 'slanted' version of a typeface. e.g. *italic*
Justified	The aligning of text so that the left and/or right sides of the text are in line. Variations—left justified, right justified or fully justified. The latter uses spacing to ensure that each line is justified on both the left and right, thus making them all the same length.
Layout	This is the arrangement of type and graphic elements on a page to best advantage.
Leading	This is also known as line spacing and refers to the spacing between each line of text. This is a term left over from old methods of setting type when lead was used to space the lines accurately.
Lower case	This is the version of characters that are not capitals or upper case. e.g. abcdefghijklmnopqrstuvwxyz
Margin	This is the empty space around a column of type or around an entire page.
Noun	A noun is the name of a person, place or thing.
Object	This is the noun in a sentence that receives the action being performed by the subject of the sentence.
Orphan	This is a single word or opening line of a paragraph separated from the rest of the paragraph, commonly at the foot of a page.
Point	This is the traditional measurement of a typeface size. There are 72 points in one inch.

Prelims	'Prelims' stands for 'preliminary pages'. These precede the main text of a publication and include the title page, imprint, Preface, Foreword and Contents.
Preposition	This is the word placed before a noun to show its relation to other words or their function in a sentence.
Proof	This is a trial copy of a typeset publication for the purpose of checking and correction.
Proofreading	This is the final quality check of a document including the checking of typesetting and layout and is often performed against the original copy.
Pull-Quotes	These are phrases or quotes set off in quotation marks or some other treatment. It is used to attract a reader's attention.
Question mark	This is the mark placed at the end of a sentence, which indicates that the sentence is a question. e.g. ?
Recto	This is the right-hand (odd-numbered) page in a book.
Roman	This is the normal, upright, non-slanted type of a font. e.g. Roman
Running footer & Running header	This is a brief descriptive heading that often appears at the bottom or top of every page.
Run on	This causes sentences to follow each other without a paragraph break or other break.
Sans-serif	Fonts designed without finishing strokes are called 'sans-serif' fonts. They have straight stems and clean lines. e.g. Arial.
Script	This is a font type based on ornate writing. e.g. *Script*
Sentence case	Each main word starts with a capital letter. Small words – eg. of, the, a – are not capitalised.
Serif	This is a finishing stroke on the end of the stem of a character. Times New Roman is a common example of a serif font.
Small caps	These are small sized uppercase letters, generally set to the size of the main part of a lowercase character in the same font, e.g. THIS IS SMALL CAPS, THIS IS NORMAL CAPS.
Solidus	This a forward slash. e.g. /.
Stem	This is an upright stroke in a character.
Subject	The subject is the noun in a sentence about which something is said.
Title page	This page contains the full title of the book, any subtitle, the name(s) of authors, coordinating editors and translators, the edition and the publisher's name and logo.
Typesetting	This is the process of formatting a manuscript to have an appealing and easy to read layout, according to its intended audience and use.
Upper case	This is the version of a character that is a capital letter. e.g. ABCDEFGHIJKLMNOPQRSTUVWXYZ
Verb	A verb is the action word or words in a sentence.
Verso	This is the left-hand (even-numbered) page of a book.
Widow	This is the short last line of a paragraph at the top of a page.

Now what?

Okay now you've determined that you are made of the stuff proofreaders need to be made of and you have all the tools needed to start work as a proofreader. Except one thing – the specific knowledge of the proofreader's language.

As we've seen, the proofreader's job is to check manuscripts for errors and indicate the changes necessary to fix them. To do this they use a two-pronged marking system, placing marks on a hard copy of the proof.

The basic technique employed entails marking the error within the text in the required way and then placing the correction in the margin.

Thinking of words as patterns, rather than words, helps you to determine which instruction to use to enable the easiest and clearest marking, and thus avoid any misunderstandings by the layout designer. So, don't think first that a misspelt word is wrongly spelled, think first that the pattern of letters is incorrect, and then overlay the possibility of a misspelt word. Once you determine the spelling that is necessary, you will be able to see the best way to correct the mistakes in the pattern of the word. It's not as confusing as it sounds, and in the end makes for easier marking up of proofs.

This thinking can be applied to any type of layout, any type of document.

The Proofreader's Language

The proofreader uses specific mark-up symbols as a shorthand method for indicating what needs to be done to fix any problems that are found. You may already use a few of these as some are in common use.

As stated earlier, because the text has little space between each line it is necessary to break up the instructions to the layout designer by indicating where in the text a problem exists and exactly what is in error and then place the required fix in the margin.

Never assume that the layout designer is grammar literate or can spell or knows anything about punctuation. They may and may even be better at such things than you are, but the manner in which they work does not necessarily enable them the luxury of seeing when these elements are wrong or the best way to fix them.

In a standard book the proofreader uses the left hand margin to place the change instructions for the left hand side of the page and the right hand margin to place the instructions for the right hand side of the page. This means the proofreader imagines a line down the middle of each page and uses this as a guide for which margin to use. Likewise, this is how the layout designer will identify what changes belong to which text mark.

In a non-fiction document that may contain graphics of various types and/or columns, in other words, special layouts, the proofreader must be more flexible with margin marks and often using the white space between elements is the best option treating these as if they are margins.

The marks in the margin are placed from left to right as the errors appear in each half of the page and as we commonly read. Here is an example of a few lines of text with their proofreading markings.

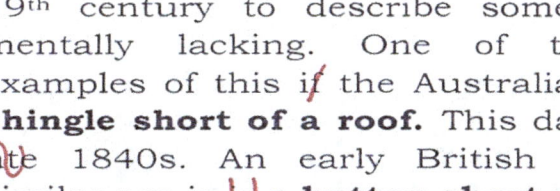

The markings for each line must be placed beside that line so it is clear for the layout designer where the marks belong. Therefore, you must leave enough room for multiple markings on each half of the page. The left hand margin markings must be away from the text, starting in from the edge of the paper perhaps 1cm and the markings on the right hand side of the page must be away from the text sufficiently to be clear of the text and not be missed. This is particularly important if the right hand side is not justified.

It is often easier to think of the text you are proofreading as patterns of characters rather than words as such. If you look for the incorrect patterns you will be able to spot much more than spelling mistakes – such things as missing punctuation, inconsistent formatting, missing words, incorrect spacing, missing or extra matter.

Every page and every mark on every page needs to be proofread, including title pages, imprint page, headers, footers, headings.

Particularly check things like page numbers for correct order, chapter/section numbering for continuity, and that headers and footers are as per style sheet or instructions.

Now that you know the methods used by a proofreader, it's time to learn the special language used to mark up proofs.

How do I replace something that is wrong?

How do I replace characters that are wrong?

One of the easiest errors to spot is when a character or group of characters is incorrect. Or at least you would think so. It is mostly, once you train your brain to not auto correct the small errors that you see. Our brains are actually wired to do this, but practise makes it very possible to change the way you see things and actually spot those errors that you would normally just skip over and not notice when you are reading.

So, let's look at the way we mark-up replacing/changing any incorrect characters that you spot.

To change a single character place a **/** through the wrong character.

> Example: this

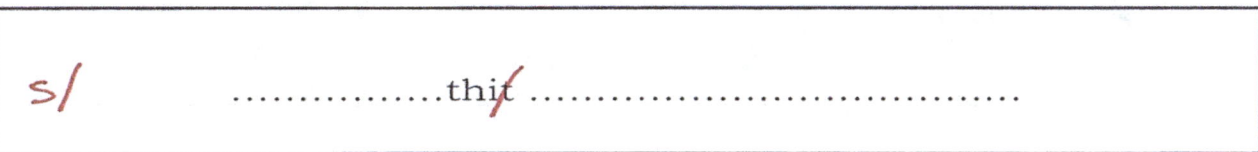

Next you need to place the correct character in the margin, according to which half of the page the error occurs. Remember the imaginary line down the middle of the page. If the change needed is on the left half of the page, you need to insert it in the left hand margin area. Place it away from the text so there is room for further marks for that line if necessary. If it is in the right half of the page then place the correction in the right margin leaving a small gap for clarity purposes. If the lines are not right justified, then make sure you place the correction past the longest line, otherwise it may be missed if it actually has some text too close to it.

Print the required correction clearly and neatly. Do not join up characters as this can lead to misinterpretation. Then place a solidus (slash – /) after the characters (on the right hand side of your inserted characters) as so:

> **s/**

This indicates that each particular change is complete.

Multiple margin markings could look like this:

> **t/b/h/**

Practical Proofreading

If several characters are incorrect, bracket the characters as follows, with the correction in the margin, placing a vertical line through the first faulty character and the last faulty character and joining the two with a horizontal line.

    Example: characters

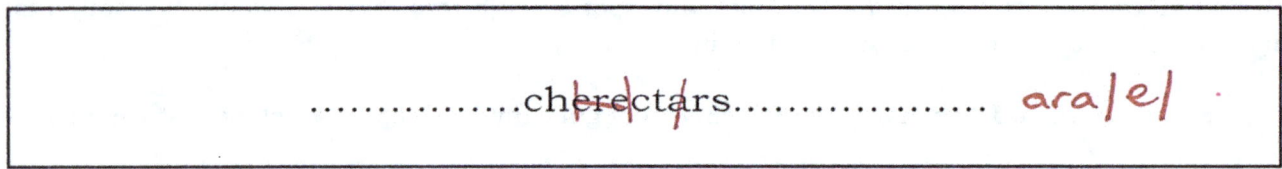

Use this method also if there are multiple single character changes as it is clearer for the layout designer to know what is required.

    Example: characters

Some special characters have specific requirements when replacing them and they are described in later sections.

    Example:

i/	Stir the liquad until it becomes smooth and creamy.
ix/	Note: Do not work the meeture too much or it will go stiff.

This is what the changes would look like after the layout designer has completed his changes.

    Stir the liquid until it becomes smooth and creamy.

    Note: Do not work the mixture too much or it will go stiff.

To replace whole words, we use the |--| bracketing method. For clarity you can include a space at the start and end of your margin change. We use the hash (#) character to indicate a space.

    Example:

How do I replace something that is wrong?

Now here is a small exercise for you to try.

The solutions for all mini exercise are at the end of the book starting at page 149.

> What makes a stary? Good questun, you say, what does make a story?
>
> A story occurs whan a protijonixt (hero) is taken out of their normal rootine world and given a problem to solve, a goal to achieve. In solving this problem they undergo change and groe and at the end of the story are different to what they were at the beginning. They experiance conflicts from external and internal influences (conflicts here being obstacles in their way). There is generally an antagonist – someone or something – that puts the externill barriers in their way, often with the same, but opposing goal, as the hero.

How do I insert missing characters or words?

How do I insert missing characters or words?

When you find that there are missing characters or blocks of characters (words), you first have to indicate where the missing matter is within the text, using the insert carat, which looks like this – ∧ .

Example: t∧e

Place the stick of the carat between the characters which need to be either side of the missing matter, with the leg portion (the upside down V) resting below the line of text. This precisely places the missing text so the layout designer knows where it belongs.

Print the missing matter in the appropriate margin, clearly and neatly. Do not join up the characters as this can lead to misinterpretation. Then place a solidus (slash – /) after the characters (on the right hand side of your inserted characters) as so -

i.e. h/

thus, indicating that the change is complete.

Example:

> **How do you create tension?**
>
> Tension is very important in a plot. To create tension need to unfold your plot slowl You need to keep the reders guessing about what will happen, keep them wating. Make possible for them to see two or three possible paths solutions to the plot.

This is what the text should look like:

How do you create tension?

Tension is very important in a plot. To create tension you need to unfold your plot slowly. You need to keep the readers guessing about what will happen, keep them waiting. Make it possible for them to see two or three possible paths or solutions to the plot.

Now let's have a little practise at inserting characters.

> **OUR SECRET LOVE**
>
> We shared secret love, full furtive looks, fleting hand touches, and not walking home opposite direction.

29

Practical Proofreading

How do I insert or replace punctuation and spaces?

Inserting punctuation is done in much the same way as inserting other matter, with the carat to indicate the position of the missing punctuation and the missing punctuation placed in the margin areas as appropriate. However certain punctuation marks need to be place in a circle to make it clear for the layout designer.

The following punctuation characters are placed in a circle:

- The full stop –
- The comma –
- Semi colon –
- Colon –
- Exclamation mark –
- Ellipses –
- Question mark –

A space is inserted in the same way as other characters, with the carat between the characters within the text but the **#** is used to indicate the needed space.

If you need to indicate that more than one of the same character is needed you can do this by adding **n x** before or **x n** after the character in the margin (where 'n' is the number required). This is often used for indicating multiple spaces.

    i.e. **# x 3/** or **3 x #/**

    Example:

> Generally things are a 'few' or 'couple' short as in a **few bricks short of a load** or a **couple of alps short of a range**

How do I insert missing characters or words?

Now it's your turn to do a mini exercise.

> No one knew but us Itwas difficult but delicious, too Our little secret, punctuated with beating hearts anda longing deep enough to giveme cramps every time our eyes met. Like now.
>
> "Oh, get a room you two" chorused the class, We both blushed Maybe our secret love was notso secret afterall.

The apostrophe, start and end quotation marks are treated as superscript characters and treated differently. A description follows further on in this manual.

How do I insert or replace dashes?

There are three types of dashes that are used in publishing. These are: the hyphen, the en-dash and the em-dash.

You will have seen all three of these at times in your reading but may not have really registered them.

However, each of them has a different use and is read differently within a piece of writing. We largely read them instinctively, even if we do not really know their true function.

The hyphen (-) is used to add a prefix to a word, or to create compound words or terms.

> Example:
>
> pre-emptive, Melbourne-Sydney railway

The en-dash is a slightly longer dash; in fact, it is the length of the letter 'n' in any given font (–). It is used to link elements in a sentence.

> Example:
>
> This was not right – just not right at all.

The em-dash is slightly longer again; it is the length of the 'm' in any given font. It is used to separate elements in a sentence or when speech is interrupted.

> Example:
>
> "I don't—" Jessica stopped as Sam interrupted her.

Practical Proofreading

To mark up a change to a dash we use the / to replace an incorrect dash or the ∧ to insert a missing dash within the text and then the dash type – en, em, or hyphen (-) in a cup as shown in the example following.

    Example:

A few wanks short of an orgasm. / not all there	[en]/
A stubbie/can short of a six pack. ∧ missing some sense	[en]/

For some practise, here is another mini exercise:

Instructions: All dashes should be en-dashes.

Short of a sheet of bark.	– weak of intellect
A few tiles short of a roof.	slow, not very quick
Ten sheep short of a top paddock.	— kind of slow, an idiot
A few French fries short of a Happy Meal.	- not too bright

How do I insert or replace other special characters?

There are a number of characters that need to be handled in a slightly different manner.

The insert carat is still used to indicate where in the body of the text the character or characters should be inserted, and the left and right hand margins are still used according to which half of the page these special characters need to be inserted into. However, how they are indicated in the margin differs.

These special characters include:

The apostrophe

The apostrophe is indicated by using the superscript indicator – ⁷.

So, when we place the apostrophe instruction in the margin it looks like this: ⁷/

How do I insert missing characters or words?

Example:

> ỷ/   Where̬s ....

The layout designer would change it to this.

> Where's .....

Single speech marks

Single speech marks are similar to apostrophes but when they are entered as a pair then each half is the opposite of the other.

> i.e. Opening speech mark ⷢ/ and, closing speech mark ⷤ/.

Note that the closing speech mark looks the same as the apostrophe, but we consider it to be a different character.

Notice the curvature of the marks in the 'bowl' of the superscript mark. This is important in order to avoid confusion, especially if many quote marks are being used, in heavily dialogued scenes. Curving the marks in the correct direction gives the layout designer notice that there are pairs of marks and if they become mismatched then they can check to see where they may have missed one or added one in that was not needed.

To change an incorrect speech mark, simply use the / through the mark needing to be changed and then place the correct mark in the margin.

Example:

> 'No, I don't want to go!/   ⷤ/

This would then change to the following when the layout designer applies the changes.

> 'No, I don't want to go!'

Double speech marks

A common mistake is to think of each of the strokes of a double speech mark, or quotation mark, as individual characters. They are not. Double speech marks are one character, so marking one of the strokes for deletion to make a single quote mark is incorrect; the whole character needs to be replaced. To indicate double quote marks use the following:

> i.e. opening – “/ , closing – ”/

Practical Proofreading

Example:

> Food metaphors are the most common, such as "a few bites short of a bickie", or a "couple of bangers short of a barbie".

Now have a go and see what you can spot needs changing.

> **Where has all the Colour Gone?**
>
> Violet woke up and looked around her bedroom. Something was wrong. It was morning. "The sun is up, but wheres my colourful bedroom?
> She pulled back her curtains. Everything outside was dull and grey, too.
> She ran to find her parents. They were listening to the news. 'The police believe the theft is the work of the Grey Witch. Anyone with information regarding this crime should contact the police on 000.

Superscript characters

Any character can be input as a superscript character. The indicator we use to tell the layout designer that a character is superscript is:

The most common you may come across is the squared or cubed mathematical expression.

Example:

> The builder needed 22 metres of timber.

This would appear in the text like this:

> The builder needed 2^2 metres of timber.

Another use for superscript is in references.

Here is an exercise in changing characters to *superscript*.

> 'The Egyptians used lapis lazuli to represent Heaven.'1
>
> ―――――――――――――――――――――――
>
> 1 www.crystal-cure.com, *Amerindea Crystal-cure, Color meaning*, 2004.

Subscript characters

Subscript characters use a similar mark to the superscript except upside down.

i.e.

They are commonly used for scientific notations.

Example:

> The chemical formula for carbon dioxide is CO2.

The result of this would be:

> The chemical formula for carbon dioxide is CO_2.

Here is a small exercise in *subscript* text changing.

> Similarly, subscripts are also used frequently in mathematics to define different versions of the same variable: for example, in an equation $x0$ and xf might indicate the initial and final value of x, while $v$rocket and $v$observer would stand for the velocities of a rocket and an observer. Commonly, variables with a zero in the subscript are referred to as the variable name followed by "nought" (e.g. v_0 would be read, "v-nought").

Practical Proofreading

Here are a couple of other small exercises for you to do.

> What is the cube of 30? i.e. 30_3
>
> Answer: 27,000
>
> The backyard is 5m2.
>
> The formulas for the following are:
>
> > Hydrogen peroxide—H_2O2
> > Hydrogen—H2
> > Dichlorine Hexoxide—$CI2O_6$

Space or spaces between blocks of characters (words)

Spaces between characters are indicated in the margin with a hash character.

    i.e. #/

To indicate insertion of more than one space, add the number of spaces required as follows:

    i.e. # x 2/ or 2 x #/

Example:

> The plot is what actually happens in the enactment of this story. Without a goal and conflicts, a story does not exist.

Another exercise for you to try.

> Everybook must have a problem to solve, or goal to achieve, whether itisa stand-alone book or part of a series. The protagonist must change fromthe start of the book to the end of the book, for the better, preferably. Thisoccurs through the conflicts the protagonist encounters, learns fromand defeats.

How do I insert missing characters or words?

How do I insert a tab at the start of a paragraph?

Indents at the beginning of lines

If a line needs to be indented, use the indent character, ⌐ , in both the text and margin.

    Example:

> ⌐ /   This is the time for all good men to come
>   to the aid of the party.

This would become: (We will presume the designer has appropriate instructions for this indent to be 5 spaces.)

        This is the time for all good men to come
   to the aid of the party.

This can be further qualified by adding a number of spaces to the margin mark.

    i.e. ⌐ x 10/

This would turn out to be:

        This is the time for all good me to come
   to the aid of the party.

If indents have been specified in the Style Sheet the layout designer will use the definitions provided to indent appropriately in the context of the design.

    Example:

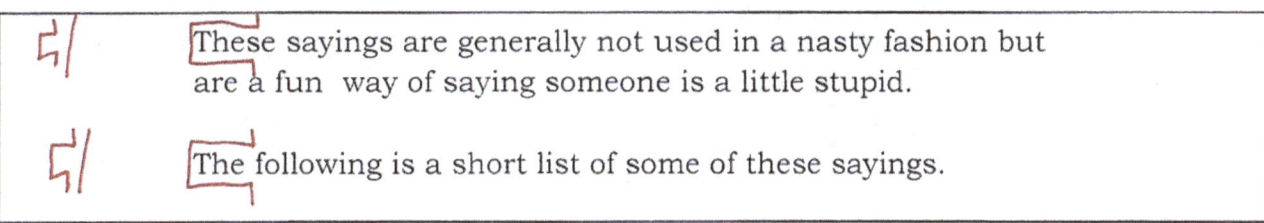

> ⌐/   These sayings are generally not used in a nasty fashion but
>   are a fun way of saying someone is a little stupid.
>
> ⌐/   The following is a short list of some of these sayings.

How do I indicate the need for a new paragraph?

Sometimes paragraphs can be run together, and it is necessary to indicate where the paragraph should be broken in two (or more). This can happen if a global change is made, or if edit changes have been missed by the layout designer.

To indicate that a paragraph needs to be inserted there is no need to indicate the exact layout, as the format of a paragraph will be contained within the Style Sheet. (If a Style Sheet is not available then it should be evident from the rest of the document).

Within the text, at the point where the new paragraph needs to start, we place the ⌊ mark around the first character of the sentence.

> Example:
>
> This is the time for all
> to come to the party.
> ⌊The time is now.

In the margin we place:

which you can guess is short for <u>N</u>ew <u>P</u>aragraph. We place the 'np' in a circle to indicate that this is an instruction and not text needing to be inserted.

> Example:

As can be seen there are as many non-slang ways of expressing stupidity as there are slang forms.

⌊Anything that has a collection of something can be used to form a 'short of' saying. ⌊Try making some up. They are fun and easy. But if you do, or if you know of others not on this list, please send them to the author so I may add them to my list.

This marking up results in the following being done:

As can be seen there are as many non-slang ways of expressing stupidity as there are slang forms.

Anything that has a collection of something can be used to form a 'short of' saying.

Try making some up. They are fun and easy. But if you do, or if you know of others not on this list, please send them to the author so I may add them to my list.

If an indent is actually the start of a paragraph, then I tend to use the **np** instruction rather than the indent instruction. This ensures that all paragraph features are completed by the layout designer. The indent instruction is most useful if indenting text or words within a paragraph or element on the page.

Often either will result in the same look but if there are things like a blank line before the paragraph, it may be missed if you indicate an indent.

How do I insert blank lines between text?

To insert blank lines between lines of text you need to use a large greater than or less than sign to indicate where the lines should be inserted (> <) and then in the margin indicate how many lines are needed.

i.e. **2x#/** or **#/** for one line.

Place the point of the sign at the insertion point to ensure that it is clear exactly where the line/s need to be inserted. This mark can be placed on either the right hand side (use the less than sign – <), or the left hand side (use the greater than sign – >).

Example:

	A few crumbs short of a biscuit.	- *neuron impaired*
#/	A few sausages short of a BBQ.	Ditto
	Several palings short of a fence.	Ditto
	A few chops short of a barbie.	- *not all there*

Practical Proofreading

Now this exercise requires you to decide what needs to be a new paragraph, what needs to be indented and where blank lines might need to be inserted. Our style sheet specifies that a new paragraph is automatically indented and produces a blank line before it. You don't need to specify each of these actions.

> 'I don't know what we'll do,' said Mum. 'The Rainbow Wizard was the only one who could fix it before, but he's gone.'
> Violet started to cry.
>
> Mum and Dad hugged her. 'It's all right,' said Dad. 'The colours will come back.' Violet's day was awful. No one could concentrate without colours. The teachers were grouchy, and the children were naughty

A note about major exercises

Now we are about to embark upon the first of our major exercises.

The major exercises in this book build on each as we go through, first concentrating on those mark-up instructions that have just been introduced and then adding in marks that have been previously learnt.

To help I have provided some instructions, a little like a mini style sheet, for those aspects that are not immediately apparent.

I have also set out each page on a yellow shaded background to simulate a page of paper, and to help with things like centred titles etc.

In reality, you would be sent A4 sized pages that would have each printed book page centred on one A4 sheet and sometimes crop marks to mark the edges of the book page.

It is generally an accepted practice that widows and orphans, are eliminated, so make sure that you handle those properly in the later exercises.

Ignore the blue page numbers of *this* book, but there may be page numbers on the exercises, so you will need to check that these are correct.

The first page of each major exercise will include the mini style sheet so will be slightly condensed in size.

Major exercise 1

- Headings – bold, centred, all capitals, blank line after.
- Paragraphs – First paragraphs in each section are full out to margin.
- Subsequent paras – indented, no blank line before.
- Page numbers – at outside margin, bottom.

HOMELESS

He was tired, tired and hungry. He sat dwn on the cold concrete. his back against the lamppost.

People rushed past him. He wondered where they were all going in such a hurry. The traffic behind him was deafening with the honking of horns, the revving of engines.

Few people noticed the man sitting quietly on the ground as they rushed past. Those did looked at his dirty clothes and sunken face with distaste. No one understood.

The man watched the clocks above the station entrance. His eyes focused on the one telling the current time. He watched the second hand move precisely around the face. As he watched, the people and cars disappeared. There was only the clock — the second hand and ticking he could so clearly hear.

The ticking matched the beating of his heart. The hands kept travelling unrelentingly around the clock face.

1

Suddenly they stopped. There was no longer any sounds, no longer rushing people and impatient cars.

At two a.m. the ambulence officers loaded his stiff cold body into the back of their ambulance. Another John Doe was added their list

2

Major exercise 2

- Headings – bold, sentence case, centred.
- Quotation marks – single
- Paragraphs – First – full out to margin.
- Subsequent paras – indented, no blank line before.

A Big Lady with a Big Heart

Her voice is touched with a light Kiwi accent She was born under the star sign Sagittarius on 12th December 1959, in Murupara not far from Rotorua, New Zealand. She describes herself as "big, brave, determined, relentless, passionate, lovable, honest and seeking'. She is sentimental, and her favourite film is *The Sound of Music*. She dotes on her family, and enjoys spending time talking with her children, Emma – fifteen, and Catherine – seven. Her adored husband is Ben, aged forty-six. She has two brothers, one of which she is close to; the other was always mean to her. She loves *Dr Phil* and *Oprah*. Her favourite book is *Jonathan Livingston Seagull* which 'expanded her wings, allowing her to explore life outside her own little box'. She has now spent more time in Australia than in New Zealand. She migrated twenty-four years ago and is an Australian citizen, because she wanted to be able to vote, something she had never been able to do in her own country. She lives in South Morang but would prefer a more open. country abode.
    Her name - is Patricia.
    In order to give her children good choices in their lives Patricia is striving to provide them with good educations, something she missed out on herself. She says that Emma 'tries to mother her and is her reality check', whereas, Catherine is 'dynamic, wild, a cat with an enormous personality who takes risks'.
    Patricia's life is bound up in her family, leaving her limited spare time to pursue hobbies In a typical display of

her quirky sense of humour, some of her 'hobbies' include: cleaning the kitty litter tray, cuddling her cat, putting clothes on the line and ironing. If given her druthers, however, Patricia would lie in bed, reading one of her favourite books.

Patricia is full of stories. Like the one when the family decided they woold like to try the fish and chips at Rex Hunt's D'lish Fish. They were not exactly sure where it was located. Patricia insisted it was in St. Kilda. Her husband insisted it was in Port Melbourne. They drove around for a while and failed to find it. So they pulled into a service station to ask for directions. Before Ben could get out of the car, another vehicle pulled up beside them. Rex Hunt climbed out. They chated to him for a while and were directed to Port Melbourne.

Patricia says she wouldn't change anything about herself and is happy with where she is'. This is an enormous achievement.

On top of this she is pursuing a dream; a dream to write, exploring what she likes and what she does well. Like so many others she has begun the Diploma in Professional Writing and Editing. Good Luck, Patricia?

How do I remove unwanted matter?

How do I delete words or characters that are not needed?

The most common form of deleting is perhaps the need to delete a single character or a block of characters. We do this by striking through the character or characters using the single slash or bracketed slash for multiple characters as described earlier, and then placing the delete symbol in the appropriate margin.

The delete symbol is a unique mark-up sign and may take some practise for you to perfect.

i.e.

Within the text, the matter to be deleted is then struck through with a /, for one character, or bracketed by slashes connected with a line, if multiple characters.

i.e. / or /————/

Example:

> I hope you you have enjoyed this list of sayings and will endeavour to use them more often. It would bee a shame to see the 'short ofs' die as so many other slang forms have.

Now let's do an exercise for *deleting characters and words*.

> She raced home when school was finished too find out if the Grey Witch had been caught, but she hadn't been. They really needed the Rainbow Wizard.
> She thought and thought until she had an idea. Her computer would help save the world!
> The chat room buzzed. She typed in her message. 'Rainbow Wizard only hope. Everyone look for him him.' Her screen started flickering with questions, but Violet had no answers.
> Then shee remembered what her parents had told here. 'He's probably the only only colour left. Keep your eyes open.'

Practical Proofreading

How do I remove unwanted spaces?

To remove unwanted spaces. we must use a 'close up symbol', ⌒ within the text and in the margin.

Example:

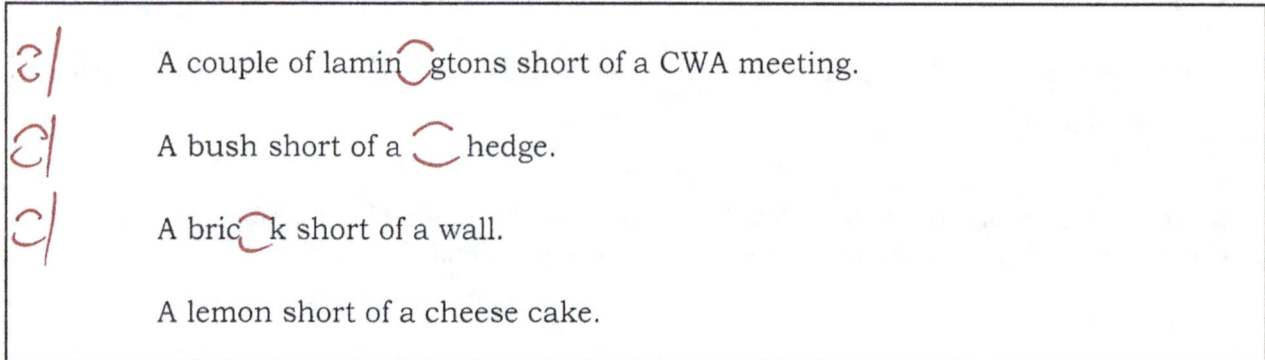

This would result in the following changes being made:

A couple of lamingtons short of a CWA meeting.

A bush short of a hedge.

A brick short of a wall.

A lemon short of a cheesecake.

If a *character* to be *deleted* is in the middle of a word, we add the close up symbol both within the text and in the margin. This makes the delete symbol look like this:

Example: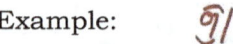

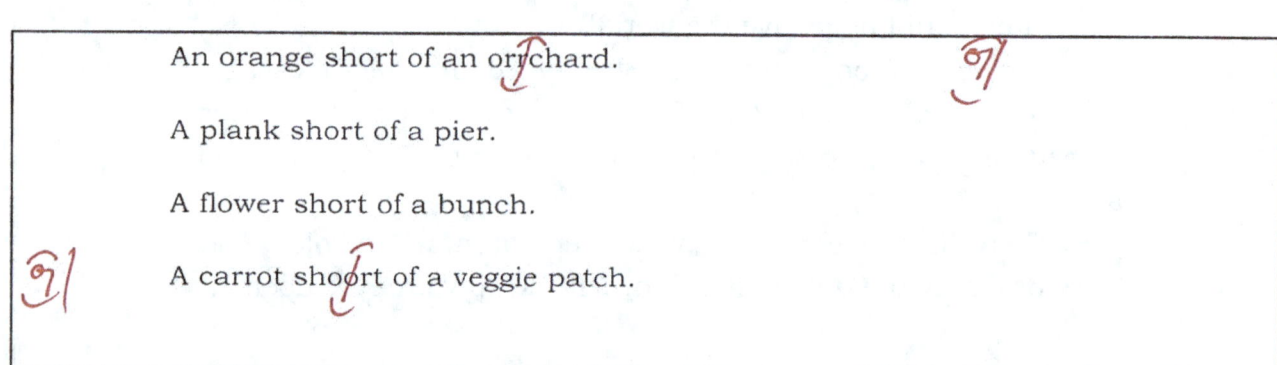

How do I delete unwanted blank lines?

To delete unwanted blank lines, we use another form of the close up symbol – **( )**. We place the two brackets at each end of the blank line, or lines, to be deleted. As we hand draw these brackets they can be as large as is necessary to clearly indicate what is required.

Example:

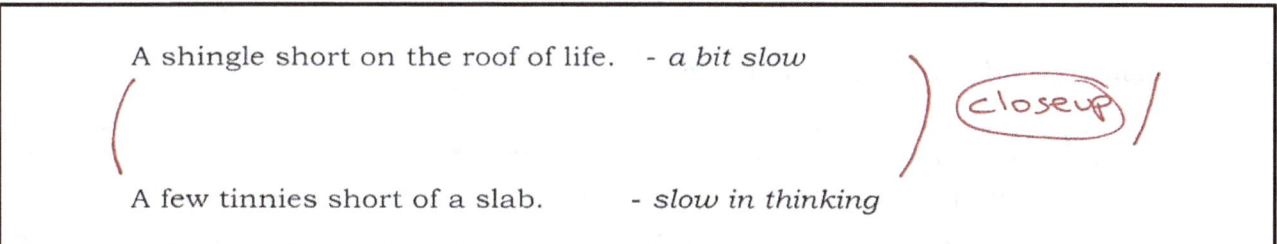

Here is an exercise to *delete unwanted spaces* between words and *remove blank lines*.

>   Children   all over the world   began looking for the Rainbow Wizard. They searched the forests, the mountains,
>
>
> and all the buildings. They went into the sewers, looked behind every door and checked the oceans. But no one found him.
>   Violet al   most gave up hope. She lay down on the grass to think and looked up at the white clouds. A patch of rainbow winked at her. She blin ked. It did it again.
>
>   She jumped to her feet and shouted, 'Rain bow Wizard we need you. Please come down.'

How do I remove a paragraph?

Sometimes a paragraph will be inserted in error. To remove a paragraph we use the 'run on' instruction. In the margin we place the words 'run on' in a circle followed by a slash, or alternatively 'r/o' in a circle – the latter being more practical as it is more compact. Place the r/o instruction beside the first of the two lines.

    i.e.   (run on)/ or (r/o)/

Within the text we use a special character that is like a snake linking the end of one line to the beginning of the next.

Practical Proofreading

Example:

> They stood, side by side,
> their linked hands joined them as one. Their hearts were as warm as the setting sun they watched go down into the ocean. The perfect end to their wedding day.

Try this mini exercise for the *run on* instruction.

> The Rainbow Wizard left his safe cloud
> and joined Violet on the ground.
> 'You have to fix the colours.'
> The Wizard shook his head.
> 'Why not?' asked Violet.
> 'Last time it made me go grey
> and dull. It took me ages to get my colour back.'
> 'But all this grey is making people go crazy. I'll help you
> find the Grey Witch and stop her for good.'

How do I delete a tab at the beginning of a line?

Another common character that may need removal is the 'tab' at the beginning of a line. This is also treated in a specific manner.

Within the text we place the 'full out' symbol:

i.e. ⌐

This is placed at the margin.

In the margin we place the instruction – full out or f/o within a circle and followed by a slash.

i.e..   or

Example:

> Some other 'short of' sayings include:
> ⌐   A sardine short of a tin.
>
> A Tim Tam short of a packet.

50

How do I remove unwanted matter?

Now try an exercise on the *full out* instruction.

Instructions: All paragraphs should be full out.

> The wizard thought for a second.
>
> 'Okay.' He spread his arms and turned around slowly. The colours started coming back. By the time his circle was complete the wizard had lost all of his rainbow colouring.
>
> With help from the chat room, they found the Grey Witch in a cave in the Black Mountains. The Rainbow Wizard cast a spell on her so she would never be able to steal colour again.
>
> The Wizard and Violet became good friends. Gradually his colours came back. Due to Violet's quick thinking no one would have to worry about colour being stolen again.

Major exercise 3

- Headings – bold, sentence case, centred. Blank line between headings and headings and text.
- Paragraphs – First – full out to margin.
- Subsequent paras – indented, no blank line before.

Poets' Breakfast 26 June 2004
Kilmore Celtic Festival

A friend and I attended the annnual Poets' Breakfast at the Kilmore Celtic Festival held on 26th June 2004 in the Kilmore Scout Hall, Kilmore.

This was the fifth Poets' Breakfast to be held. They were started by Phil Clancy who M.C.s the proceedings. He wanted to foster local interest and talent in poetry, although he does not write poetry himself.

There are two parts to the Breakfast: readings of poet's own poetry for the Sid Cantlon Poet's Award sponsored by the Kilmore Mechanics Institute; and, basically, an open reading section where anyone can read their own or other people's poetry.

The Trophy is an interesting one. It is made from an old fence post and part of it has been left rough while part has been polished, symbolising the process   of the rough poem to the polished poem or poet. The winner of each year is engraved on brss plates attached to the main trophy and they also receive a small round polished piece of local blackwood with a brass engraved plaque. This they can keep as a happy reminder of their success.

Sid Cantlon was a local drover who worked all over Australia. He was also a poet who wrote many poems about local Kilmore identities and the area itself. He lived in a tent and loved the life.

It costs $10.00 to attend the Breakfast or you can buy a Day ticket to the Festival, at $30.00, which gains you entry to other Celtic events on the day. The $10.00 entitles you to a seat at the Breakfast. If you wish to eat, you must pay for whatever you order. Prices are reasonable and you get a nicely laid out table with white tablecloths and comfortable chairs to eat at. It is really quite well presented.

Phil Clancy kicked off the proceedings wiyh reading and then the competition entrants had their say. There were ten entrants, includingmy friend and me. They were all ages from teens to people in their seventies and equal numbers of men and

women. There was a policeman, a lady who had never read or written anything before who was reading her first poem, to poems that were written on the spot. You could tell everyone was passionate about poetry and truly enjoyed writing and reading their poetry to other people.

At the end of the competition section, each member of the audience was handed a strip of paper and asked to vote on the poet they thought was best.

While the votes being counted, people came forward and read poems written by other people, some of them written by locals who were too shy to get up themselves to poems by C. J. Dennis and Banjo Patterson. My friend and I read another poem in this section as well.

On the whole, the poetry read was mainly in a ballad style and most were about the local Kilmore area, local notable residents or personal experiences. Rhyming poems were by far the most favoured, In fact, I think there was only one poem that didn't rhyme.

Finally, the time came to find out who was to be this year's Syd Cantlon Poet's Award winner. Previous years had seen, in 2000 Don Austin; 2001 Jason

Sedgewick; 2002 and 2003 Uma Brown, take home the trophy. All three had read poems this year. After a slight drum roll, Uma Brown was announced as the winner for the third year in a row.

Assumption College Kilmore were kind enough to provide gas heaters to heat the hall and the Kilmore Scout group provided breakfast and th hall to have it in.

Next year they are considering having a Poets' Supper instead as some people are finding it hard to get to the breakfast early on the cold winter mornings. However, other activities in the Celtic Festival would then be be competing with it and it might mean some people would opt to attend some other event instead of the Poets Supper.

Since the Breakfast started, the organisers have taped the readings with a view that, one day, they would like to produce an anthology. As my husband typeset and designed my Writers Group anthology, he and I have offered to to produce an anthology this year. It woud be great if this could be an ongoing feature of the Breakfast.

All in all, it is a very fun way of enjoying poetry readings. The downside being that it happens only once a year. My friend and I will return next year, having spent some, if not all, of the next twelve months perfecting our ballad style..

Major exercise 4

- Headings – bold, all capitals, centred.
- Paragraphs – First – full out to margin.
- Subsequent paras – indented, no blank line before.
- Quotation marks – single.

THE SPECIAL BOND

I have a memory; a vague notion, of kind, sad face gasing at me over the edge of my cot. I can still feel the love and closeness in that simple acct.

I was only a month old at the time; my sister was five and my brother almost eight.

At four years old I realised Dad was missing and I tried to find out why.

'Mum why don't I have a dad like everyone else?" I looked at her, willing her to give me the answer I wanted.

My mothers face remained impassive as if to talk about my dad was to open a door she had locked long ago and forgottten where she had put the key. Mistiness clouded her eyes. 'I'm sorry, sweetie, but Daddy went away a long time ago.'

'Will he come back soon.'

'No, love, he won't.' She turned back to pealing the potatoes. 'Now go and play with your sister, like a good girl. I have to get tea ready now.' She lifted a hand to brush at the tears that threatened to fall.

Tears welled in my eyes, too, as I watched her. I could feel the grief rise from her in waves and I felt terrible that I had made her so sad.

From that time onwards I listened closely and remembered everything I heard about my father. I asked my brother and sister what they remembered, and aunties and uncles, too. And then I reached inside myself and found the rest of him.

Whenever I was troubled, I would call on him to help me. And he would come.

Somehow in that last moment of his life, when he peered at me over my cot, he created a bond between us that survived even death. When I talked to him I could see him, touch him and hear him. He was real. But only to me. And he was everything, and more, that I could ever have wished for in a father.

'I wish Emma would play with me, Dad. But she's always too busy doing her "grown up' things. She's only five years older than me. She's not grown up at all,' I pouted.

Dad was silent for a minute. 'It won't be long before you will understand what she means. Just wait a short time. I promise it will all be okay.'

'But that doesn't help me. She's such a snob!'

'Who are you calling a snob? And who are you talking to?' Emma poked her head into my room, a look of disgust on her face. 'Oh, you're not talking to "Dad" again, are you?' she taunted. She had never been able to see Dad. I think it made her angry to know that I could do something she couldn't.

'Yes, I'm talking to Dad and don't you dare say he isn't here. Because I know he is.' I jumped up, ready to defend myself.

'Oh, come off it, Joanie. You know it's all your imagination. Grow up or something. Or do you *want* to end up at the nut farm?'

'Don't you dare call me crazy? I'm not.' I flew at her, all my rage seeming to explode at once.

3

'Joan — stop!' Dad said so quietly I nearly didn't hear him. There was authority in his voice, and disapproval. I had never heard that there before. I stopped dead in my tracks.

'Let it be,' he continued now that he had my attention. 'You know I am here only for you. You can't blame Emma for not believing.'

'But she should, Dad, she should!' I insisted. I looked at Emma. She rolled her eyes. 'Well, you should!' I said too her.

'Nuts! Definitely nuts!' she muttered and fled to her own room.

'You really shouldn't do that, you know,' said Dad.

'Why? She's always so *superior*. If she only *believed*, maybe she'd be able to hear you and see you, too.'

'No, she wouldn't because *she* doesn't need me, but you do.'

I thought about that for a minute and when I looked up at Dad again, he was gone. Hee always did that, gave me something to think about and time to think about it.

He was always there for me. I could tell him anything. And I asked him about everything, too. He would explain things so I could understand. It was great! We both had the same sense of humour and we would spend hours laughing at each other's jokes.

But then it all fell apart.

When I was eighteen I met someone special. He was warm and sweet and considerate and I liked him a lot. I was a little nervous about telling Dad but in the end I told him all about him. Everything except that my special man was married,

Our first date was a wonderful evening. We drove down to the beach and walked along the shoreline, talking. After a while we grew tired and sat down to gaze out past the breakers, our hands entwined. For the first time that evening we were silent, but it was a comfortable silence, no awkwardness at all. Gradually we crept closer and, finally, we kissed. When he pulled reluctantly away, my breath was coming in shoot gasps. But I wanted more. so I turned to him and we kissed again.

I suddenly felt like we were being watched. I gently disengaged myself and looked over my companion's shoulder. My father stood their, a very disapproving look upon his face. I bristled. How dare he intrude! I had not asked him to keep an eye on me. I flung a nasty 'go away' look at him and relaxed back into the warm arms that held me. I felt safe there and welcome. There was a faint tickle of guilt trying to make itself felt in my consciousness. After all Gary *was* married. I pushed it determinedly away. This was only our first date and who knew what was going to happen? Later, when I looked, my father was gone.

For some time, I was too angry to call on my father. In fact, it was many months before I could bring myself to do so. In the meantime, my relationship with Gary deepened. His marriage broke up and we became engaged.

Then one day I woke up and felt a huge hole in my happiness. The anger I had kept towards my father was gone. I mised him very much. So I called to him to come to me. At first nothing happened. I tried again and again and again. My heart started beating almost out of control, and it was very difficult to think clearly. It had been so long our bond was almost severed.

'Daddy, please come to me. I need to talk to you,' I called frantically.

I waited. A faint form tried to appear.

"Daddy, please come. I'm sorry. I love you.' It gradually grew more solid. I waited anxiously as the form wavered back and forth between the substantial and insubstantial.

'I love you, Daddy,' I repeated, and he was there.

I ran to him and rapped my arms around him, tears streaming down my face. 'Im sorry, Daddy. I'm

7

sorry. I didn't mean to act so stupidly. I didn't mean to hurt you.'

He stroked my hair and kissed me on the forehead, like he used to do when

he comforted me when I was a little girl. He brushed the tears away from my cheeks and smiled. 'Tell me what you've been up to.'

We spoke for hours. I told him all that I had done over the last several months. And he listened to me carefully. He smiled slowly and gathered me into his arms again.

I knew then that this was the last time I would see him.

'Daddy, what's wrong? What's going on? I felt my heart quicken and my eyes opened wide with fear.

He pulled away so he could answer me properly. His eyes scanned my face as if he needed to remember every detail of what he was seeing.

'I have to go now, sweetie,' he said. He took my hands in his and kissed the back of each of them. 'I'm very proud of you. You know that, don't you?'

I noded. My heart hammered even louder.

'You know I came back because you needed me? Well, you don't need me anymore. You're strong and you're smart and you're beautiful.'

'NO, Dadddy!' I cried. 'No, you can't go. I won't let you.'

He gathered me to him again. 'You have to, sweetie. I just can't be here any more. It's not allowed. I have to rest now. I'm very tired.'

I looked at him then. I hadn't noticed before; he had always looked like he did in the photo Mum still kept on the mantelpeace. There were wrinkles round his eyes, now, and his hands were old and gnarled. My father had grown old and I hadn't noticed.

After a while he moved away, holding on only to my hands.

We held hands for as long as we could and then he was gone. He was satisfied I would be safe and happy.

And, I have been.

9

Even though my father no longer comes to me,
I know that is with me.

How do I move matter around?

What do I do if words or letters are around the wrong way?

Sometimes, perhaps due to typing mistakes, we see letters that are around the wrong way, known as 'transposed'. Sometimes it can even happen to words.

To instruct that the characters or words need to be swapped around we use a special transpose symbol, wrapped around them (⌒). Then in the margin we place the transpose instruction in a circle, like this:

i.e. (trs)/

Example:

Transposing characters:

 Back fo beoynd

Transposing words:

 Out back the of shed Barry stored his priceless collection of motorcycles, in a carport specially built purpose for the.

Now here is a small exercise for *transposing* for you to complete.

'Will stop you that?' said her mother. 'It's very annoying, and it won't make the bus get hree any quicker.' She her pulled gloves on tighter and hunkered into her thcik coat.

Practical Proofreading

How do I move text forward to the next page?

Sometimes it may be necessary to move text forward from the bottom of one page or column to the top of the next, to ensure that the relevant information is kept together for logic, flow or clarity.

To do this use the 'take over' mark, ⌐ , at the beginning of the line to be moved forward.

Then use the instruction in the margin.

Example:

The Symbolism of Colour

⌐Colours have different meanings for each of us. They

New page--

certainly mean different things in different cultures. Let's explore some of these meanings.

Red is the strongest colour. It is the colour of Mars and

How do I move text backwards?

Likewise, it may be necessary to request that a line or lines of text be moved back to a previous column or page.

You mark this in a similar fashion to moving text forward. You use the 'take back', ⌐ , mark at the end of the line to be moved backwards and the instruction in the margin.

Example:

other war gods. It is associated with fire, vitality, blood and energy. Red is the colour of passionate love, sensuality and desire. It symbolises anger and acts as a warning colour

New page--

 against danger.⌐

How do I move matter around?

Please do the following mini exercise for practise.

> Beverley stopped tapping her feet and stood up instead to give her
> New page---
> seat to an elderly woman who just joined them.
>
> Beverley began to pace up and down. She dug her hands into her pockets and went backwards and forwards. Her mother glanced heavenwards willing for the bus to turn up soon.
>
> The elderly woman sighed as she sat down. 'Was clocken det
> New page---
> buss?' she asked.

Please Note: Previous changes may affect any specified *take over* and *take back* instruction and, therefore, the Layout Designer will ultimately make the decision regarding whether these changes are required. However, by specifying the *take over* or *take back* instruction they will understand what is required.

69

Practical Proofreading

Major exercise 5

- Headings – bold, sentence case, centred. Two blank lines between heading and text.
- Paragraphs – First – full out to margin.
- Subsequent paras – indented, blank line before.

Diary of a Sleep Apnoea Sufferer

Never have I felt so epxosed before, so naked, so utterly at the mercy of these torturers.

Sure, let's go have a sleep study! Sounds simple, doesn't it? No one tells you what it's really like though. Is this really worth the pain and humiliation for a sound night's sleep, some energy and no more snoring.

I guess it is.

At least, I'm not alone. Two other ladies and a man (who is keeping to himself) are sharing this experience with me. Well, not really sharing. More like they're just here, too. With the same problems I have, no doubt, or similar anyway.

God, I wish this night were over.
Had a little pause there. It was my turn to be wired. Then, kindly, they said I could go and watch television. One of the other ladies was done before me and the other is being done now. I don't know what I look like but the lady the across room looks

1

like some sort of weird alien or robot or something. She has half a dozen wires attached to her face, a couple on her neck and one in her hair. So do I. Not what you might call fashionable.

A couple of the areas where they've stuck electrodes are still stinging. I laughed when I saw the nurse pick up a tiny piece of sand paper. I didn't for long, though. I doubt I have any skin left on my face where she rubbed it, first with alcohol and then the sand paper. A deadly combination if ever I knew one.

Somehow I dont think I'd wish this torture on my worst, or best, enemy.

All three of us have been sitting here trying to watch television as if nothing is out of the ordinary. The man elected to stay in his room. I guess we intimidated him. Good for us!

Uh, oh, the nurse just popped in to see if any of us were ready to go to bed. Not yet, we all said, but I keep thinking that maybe I should get it over with. My courage is non-existent, however, so I'll sit

2

here for a little while longer

My bladder drove me out of the chair and to the toilet and so I decided to take the plunge. But so had everyone else, so I am waiting until someone is ready to plug me in.

Well, here I am. All the wires from my head are plugged into the bed panel. I have a wire attached to each leg and they are attached as well to the bed. Then I have this bloody uncomfortable breathing thing stuck up each nostril. (The nurse said it was to measure the air coming out of my nose.) Finally, I have an oxygen monitor attached to a finger on my right hand.

How on earth am I supposed to sleep with all this garbage on? To top it all off, there is a video camera on the wall, staring straight at me. Great! No secrets for me anymore!

Time to go to sleep I guess.

I made it. It didn't take much to get to sleep,

although I can't say I slept normally. Every I time rolled over, I tangled all the wires and I was afraid I'd pull some out and then I'd have to come back and do it again. No way!

I only had to call the nurse once during the night, (although I was dead scared that I would have to get up and go to the loo, even though I don't normally), The tubes from my nose started to strangle my ears and I couldn't work out where they went to so I had to get the nurse to loosen them. I slept much better after that.

In the true form of nature and physics or whatever, it takes only a couple of minutes tops to remove all the wires from the various portions of my body.

I'm free! Hubby will here be in a few minutes so I better get dressed and pack my bag.

I probably did that in record time. My watch tells me I have time to go to the loo.

Hubby is here now. Come on, what are you

4

Practical Proofreading

waiting for. You promised me a Maca's breakfast and even if that's out, I wanna get home.

Good-bye Austin Hospital. I hope to never see you again. At least not
until I have the follow up sleep study once the official report comes back and my sleep apneoa is confirmed.

Ah, well, a good night's sleep probably is worth it!

Major exercise 6

- Headings – bold, sentence case, centred. Blank line between headings and text.
- Paragraphs – First – full out to margin.
- Subsequent paras – indented, blank line before.
- Quotation marks – single

It's Just Not Fair!

It's not fair, thought Sarah. It's just not fair! She was standing at the bus stop, waiting for the bus to Assumption College. It was the first day of Year 7. It meant a new school and being at the bottom of the ladder again.

The new school didn't worry her. Nor did being on the bottom of the ladder. But it wasn't fair that she had to go to a different school than all her friends.

'You'll meet new ones,' her mum had said, 'You wait, by the end of the first day you'll wonder why you were worried.'

She'd rolled her eyes, *Sure Mum, anything you say, Mum. But it's not you starting at a new school, it's not you being separated from your friends. It's just not fair!*

She grumpily kicked some innocent stones that were unaware of her mood or surely they would have found some way to out get of her way.

Other kids started to arrive. Kids, older,

wiser, more experienced in the way of school buses. When it finally arrived, she'd somehow ended up at the end of the queue, which wasn't fair seeing she had been the first there. She struggled up the steps with her bag. The crowded bus was full of happily chatting and, in some cases, singing kids from her age through to what looked like Year 12s. She stood at the top of the step, looking from an empty seat. The driver turned in his seat to help. After a few seconds, they both gave up. 'I'm sorry, love, but I think you'll have to stand. It's all right, thought, it's only about ten minutes to the college.'

'Thank,' she mumbled. Fat lot of good you are, she thought ungratefully.

'I'll make sure there's a seat for you tonight." She smiled and moved down the aisle a little where there was space to stand between the bags.

Just as she settled, the bus lurched, and she nearly fell onto the bags at her feet. As it was they got a little trampled.

2

'Hey watch me bag. It's got me lunch in it,' a belligerent voice shouted at her.

She crniged. This was turning into her worst nightmare.

'Give over, Jack. Can't you see it's her first day and the poor kid has to stand and all. Why don't you offer her your lap? She's not bad looking, you know,' a slightly English voice defended her in a sniggering fashion.

Sarah felt the blood rush to her face and she looked at Jack only to find him considering her. The blood then proceeded to drain from her face.

'Leave her alone guys. It hasn't been so long since you were one of the new kids. It's not fair to pick on her. Come here, I'll keep those two wolves from being nasty.' The girl who spoke was obviously someone with authority. Sarah didn't know whether Assumption had prefects or not like in Harry Potter, but if they didn't, this girl obviously had some

3

influence.

The guys started arguing and left her alone and so she moved down t where the older girl sat. There was more room on the floor there and so it was easier to stand.

'Hi, I'm Sarah McClean,' she said shyly, 'Thankyou for that.'

'Oh, it's nothing. They always try to throw you new ones. Don't listen to them. They're not dangerous or anything, just stupid. I'm Joanne Carter. If you need anything just let me know, everyone knows me. Oh, meet Joy, she's my little sister. She starts today, too. Maybe you two will end up in the same class.'

They exchange 'Hi's' but both were feeling too daunted to chat.

It seemed like forever, but bus finally arrived at the school. With her new-found friends, Sarah fought her way off and managed to get out when

4

she was meant to instead of being pushed to the back.

Joanne assured everyone her would sort themselves out over the next couple of days and getting on or off would become much more orderly.

'The start of the year is always the worst. For everyone. Not only you newies. Just make sure you stick up for yourself and you'll be all right.'
They headed into the school. Sarah thought it probably wasn't such a bad looking school but her heart still wanted to be with Nell at Whittlesea Secondary College.

Joyce noticed the downwood trend of her mouth. 'Come on, you'll be all right. There's about eighty new kids, all in the same boat as you. You'll make friends. You already know Joy. I'm sure you'll meet others.'

Sarah smiled at her gratefully but still felt like life was being terribly unfair. She had to admit that meeting Joyce and Joy was a stroke of luck, though.

'Okay you two. I think you have to go to the auditorium where you'll be classed off and from there you'll enjoy a normal hard working day like the rest of us. I'll keep an eye out for you at recess. But remember Joy I'm only babying you today. Tomorrow you're on your own.'

'Okay, okay. I don't need "babying" today, though, so don't worry about it.' A glint of unshed tears gleamed in her eyes as she was afraid her big sister would take her up on her offer.

'No way. You know I promised Mum I'd look after you. Well, I am. For today. After that you should be right.'

The two new girls followed the directions and made their way to the auditorium

It seemed crowed but Sarah found herself already feeling a little more comfortable. The classes were divided, and Sarah and Joy found

6

themselves sharing most of their subjects.

Sarah's grumpy mood was having a hard time lingering after this. And especially when she kept finding
familiar faces among the new flock. She, perhaps, couldn't put a name to them but the fish-out-of-water loneliness started to fade.

Of course, the last thing she would admit was that Mum was right!

But secondary school without her best friends looked like it might be all right after all.

She linked arms with Joy and headed off to their lockers. She was in secondary school now. None of that being led around by the hand. She had to organise herself and work hard. Maybe it wasn't fair that she had to go to a different school but maybe it was going to be okay, two.

How do I indicate how text should look?

How do I change lower case characters to capitals?

Changing lower case characters to upper case (capitals) requires the use of a unique marker within the text. Underneath the characters to be changed to capitals, insert a triple underline.

i.e. ≡

Then in the margin place either the abbreviation 'caps' or 'u/c' in a circle. Don't forget the closing slash to indicate the end of the mark.

i.e.  or

Example:

Tuesday's colour is red.

In china, it symbolises prosperity and joy, and is worn by brides.

Red gemstones help strengthen the body, promote will power, courage, add vitality, and overcome sexual dysfunctions. Appropriate red gemstones include: Red Coral, bloodstone, Garnet, red jasper, and Rubies.

Here is some practise for you to do:

> mother looked at her blankly. 'I'm sorry but i don't speak swedish,' she said, wringing her gloved hands together and, not for the first time, wishing she had taken the time to take some lessons.

How do I change capital letters to lower case?

Changing upper case characters (capitals) to lower case is easy. Within the text you simply slash through the characters needing to be lower case, either with individual slashes or the bulk slash technique of a slash through the first character and then through the last character joined by a horizontal line. Then in the margin you place the lc command in a circle.

i.e.

Practical Proofreading

Example:

Blue symbolises Youth, spirituality, truth, PEACE, water, distance, cleanliness and contemplation. It also symbolises the VIRGIN Mary, sky, ocean, sleep and twilight.

IN Greece and Rome, Blue was the colour of Zeus and Jupiter.

An exercise for changing to *lower case*.

'YOU are English?' the elderly Lady said, her accent thick.

'No. No, Australian,' saiD Mother.

How do I change ordinary text to Italics?

Italics can be used to indicate emphasis, for names of movies, plays, books, planes, boats, etc. They can also be used to indicate thoughts, time shifts and others. Check a good grammar reference for other uses.

To indicate that matter needs to be Italic, insert a horizontal line beneath the text and then place the command 'ital' in the margin.

i.e. ——— within text and in the margin.

Example:

Blue is the colour of Wednesday.

Blue gemstones are used to promote peace and calm ragged  emotions. Some blue gemstones include: Sodalite, Turquoise, Aquamarine, Blue Quartz and Lapis Lazuli.

Here's an *Ital* exercise for you to do.

Instructions: The words 'sick', the 2nd 'why', and 'forever' need to be Italicised.

'Mum when is the bus coming? I'm sick of sitting out here in the cold. Why couldn't we have got here closer to the time?' Beverley glared at her mother. 'I don't know why we couldn't have a car here. Public transport is so gay. It takes forever to get anywhere.'

How do I change Italic text to ordinary text?

'Ordinary' text is what we call 'Roman' text. This may happen by accident during the formatting process or the decision may be made to remove the emphasis from some of the text. Whatever the reason to mark up this change you need to circle the text to be changed back to Roman type, or ordinary text, within the body of the proof and then place the instruction 'rom' in the margin. You can include several words in the one circle. There is no need to circle each word individually.

i.e. ◯ around the text to be changed, and,

(rom) in the margin.

Example:

> (rom) Green has been a sign of (calamity) and evil, but has become a symbol of fate and randomness, both positive and (negative). It (rom) is associated with envy, self-respect, well-being and balance. It (rom) also symbolises (money).

Now let's try a *Rom* exercise. Turn all the italicised text back to Roman.

> 'Dear, the bus is only *about* five minutes away now. Then we'll be able to get on our way. You know they changed the timetable on us; otherwise we would have been on the bus already. And you know that we decided it was *cheaper* for us to *forget* about a car while we were here and safer, too, considering we know *nothing* about driving in the snow.' Mother's *face* had turned bright red.

How do I change text to be bold or bold text to ordinary text?

At times text may need to be in bold face type, usually to provide some sort of emphasis or to make it more visible for some reason.

To change any text to bold you need to place a horizontal wavy line underneath the text to be changed and place the instruction 'bold' in the margin.

i.e. 〰 within the text and (bold) in the margin.

Practical Proofreading

Sometimes text may be bolded by accident. In this case you will need to indicate that the text be un-bolded. To do this, place a wavy horizontal line under the text to be un-bolded and the 'unbold' instruction in the margin.

i.e. ～～ in the text and (unbold) in the margin.

Example:

Friday is **green** day.

Green gemstones promote growth and fertility, attract money, prosperity and wealth. The following gemstones are used in this way: Emerald, Malachite, Aventurine, Jade, Peridot, **Moss Agate**, Chrysoprase and Serpentine.

Let's have a go at doing a small exercise in *bolding* and *un-bolding* text.

Instructions: 'holiday' is the only word that should be bold.

The **elderly** lady ignored her reaction to Beverley's rudeness. Instead she continued as if they had not been interrupted, her original question having already been answered.

'Are you here on holiday?' the old **lady** asked, in her heavily accented but almost perfect English.

How do I indicate text should be underlined?

Indicating that text should be underlined is done by placing a horizontal line underneath the text that should be underlined and then placing the instruction 'u/l' or 'underline' in the margin, in a circle as usual.

i.e. ―― in the text and in (underline) the margin.

Example:

(u/l) x4/ **Yellow** suggests betrayal, cowardice and fear. According to David Fontana in his book *The Language of Symbols* it is the sacred colour of the Emperor in China, and to Buddhists it means humility. It is the colour symbolic of sickness.

88

Now let's do an exercise on *underlining* text.

Instructions: All occurrences of Ericsson's, Mother, lady and Beverley need to be underlined.

> 'No, my husband works for Ericsson's. He has a contract here.' Mother spoke slowly and clearly. It was always difficult to know how much English people knew but she could always count on it being more than the Swedish she knew.
>
> 'How long will you be here?' the old lady continued. She smiled warmly at Mother, ignoring Beverley completely.

How do I centre text?

Some text may have been designed to be centred, such as headings, captions to pictures or illustrations, maybe even small quotes.

If something has not been centred you will need to indicate that the text needs to be, by placing the special brackets on each side of the text to be centred and then place the 'centre' instruction in the margin.

i.e.  around the text and  in the margin.

Example:

 ⌈Sunday's colour is yellow-gold.⌉

Yellow gemstones are used to promote the ability to express oneself. They are excellent gems for writers and public speakers to increase eloquence and mental awareness. Some yellow gemstones include: Amber, Citrine, and Imperial Topaz.

Now a short exercise. The heading here needs to be *centred*.

The Bus Stop

The bus was still fifteen minutes away. Beverley tapped her feet and gazed around.

Practical Proofreading

How do I make sure lines start in the same place?

At times it may be necessary to indent a whole paragraph or section of text, for example, when a large quote is inserted from another source, or it may just be a design choice for a particular part of the document.

If this indentation has been missed, or in other words if text is not aligned as desired, use a vertical line at the position where the text should be aligned and the 'align' instruction in the margin.

    i.e. ‖ in the text and in (align)/ the margin.

Example:

| It is associated with spring, Easter, harvest, and is used to warn of potential danger. It is the colour of the sun, of light, of summer. Yellow can also mean wisdom, joy and happiness. |

Time for an *aligning* exercise.

| 'About two years, we think.' She shifted on her seat and looked up the road in the direction of the bus. |
| 'That is a great adventure,' said the old lady. |
| 'Yes. Tell Beverley that,' muttered Mother. |

Major exercise 7

- Headings – First line – Bold, centred, all capitals
- Headings – Second line - bold, sentence case, centred. One blank line after headings.
- Paragraphs – First – full out to margin.
- Subsequent paras – indented, no blank line before.

Holiday Haunts to Die For

From The Spirits Travel Agency Inc.

I bet you've just died for a holiday. After your full haunting training you probably need something for your tired spirit. Here are the Top Five Holidays of Bad Luck for the haunting exhausted ghost.

first on our tour is the famous Death Valley, California, USA. The ghost towns have a social life that can't be beaten. The best spot in the valley is Ballarat named after an Australian goldmining camp. Catch up with some famous spooks and get some tips from the best. Accommodation is no problem once the living are scared off and then it's spiritual bliss for the weary.

MOVing on to Tombstone, Arizona, will just turn your poltergeist inside out. *Watch* the re-enactment at the O.K. Corral - by the original participants. Be warned, keep your thoughts to yourself or you may find yourself in more than a re-enactment of one of the bloodiest episodes in the West. But maybe that's the excitement you are looking for. If you want a quieter time, be entertained by living as the local dead play their tricks.

The USA offers a plethora of other ghostly and magical places to visit. You might want to make a side trip before moving on with the rest of your tour. Let your agent know and I am sure you will have trouble deciding where to go.

Our next stop is the Dead Sea This is a bit of a jump from California to Israel, but, hey! We're not ghosts for nothing! The big attraction here is that even ghosts can float in the waters. The black mud baths should not be missed. They lift the most flagging of spirits. Situated 400 meters below sea level, it brings to life the heat of Satan's fires.

Another highly recommended vacation is a cruise on the Titanic. Bored of its Atlantic runs, it has been travelling between Europe and Australia for nearly half a century. It is a wonderful deep-sea experience featuring seaweed-shrouded cabins, rotting timbers and rusting hull.

Our stop final before returning to our respective haunts, is Queen Victoria Market, Melbourne, Australia. Unknown to most of the living this is one of the largest ex-cemeteries in the Southern Hemisphere. Many of the 10,000 souls buried
here are experts in their haunting and use some of the most refined techniques ever employed. For those who wish an intellectual challenge this can be a real learning haunt.

I'm sure everyone will be able to find something interesting amongst these Five Top Ghostly Holidays, from phantasm to ghost. Cotss are kept low with our tours as you use your own powers to travel. We look after all other details. So, with a little planning you need never have an unenjoyable holiday again. After all you'll be in this **afterlife** for a very long time.

Major exercise 8

- Heading – bold, sentence case, centred. Blank line between heading and text.
- Paragraphs – First – full out to margin.
- Subsequent paras – indented, no blank line before.
- Speech marks – double.

The Tale of Little Red Riding Hood

red stole from the sleeping house and disappeared into the dark city streets. She gathered her red coat close and buried her head in its hood. Her grandmother lived on the other side of the city.
She had been walking for quite some time when she ran into a strange man. He introduced himself as Mr Wilbur Wolfe and asked why she was out alone so late at night.

    Red though tiny in stature, was as **bold** as they come. She straightened up and looked him in the eye. Her grandmother was ill and she was going to look after her. Little did he know that she was actually running away from home. Her parents had finally gone too far. They wouldnt let her do anything she knew her friends did.

    Mr Wolfe bade her good night and be careful. He headed off down Union Street. Red continued down Main Street, where she loved to look in the shop windows and dream about buying everything she wanted.

    Wolfe hurried and found Red's grand mother's house before Red had gone past her first store. He knocked and when grandmother answered, he adopted a high-pitched voice pretending to be Red needing to talk to her urgently.

    Grandmother opened the door. Mr Wolfe pushed her inside, threatening her with a gunn in his pocket. He bound and gagged her and locked her in a cupboard. He put on some of Grandmother's clothes and makeup and practiced her croaky voice. It wouldn't be Red looking after her grandmother tonight; he had plans to look after Red.

A little time passed, and he start to grow bored. Then a knock sounded on the front door.

"It's me, Grandma,' called Red.

"Come in, dear. I'm in the lounge room," croaked Wolfe in his best grandmother voice.

Red thought her grandmother looked a little odd when she found her, but she was too upset with her own problems to wonder about her grandmother's looks.

"What is the matter, dear? It's very late for a visit, you know. " Wolfe gestured for her to come closer and patted the seat beside him on the couch.

"It's horrible, Grandma, Mum and Dad won't let me do anything. It's so unfair. Can I come and live with you?"

"Well, that sounds like a good idea. I'm sure we could be very happy living together."

Red grew suspicious. She looked closer.

"Grandma, your ears are all hairy. I've never noticed that before."

"Well, dear, I'm taking a special tonic to give me energy and it's made the hair in my ears grow."

"Oh," said Red. "And your eyes look bigger and brown. I always thought you had blue eyes."

"That's my cataracts acting up. But they're all right."

"Grandma have you been working out. Your arms

look very muscly."

'Oh, yes, thank you, my dear. I have been exercising a little. It helps me with carting the firewood."

"And Grandma, your hands seem bigger than they used to be. Are they all right?"

"Oh, yes dear. They need to be so I can hold onto you when you struggle."

Red realised she was trouble but knew what to do. They'd had classes on this at school. She jumped up.

Wolfe jumped up, too, and lunged at her. She dodged, stuck out her foot, and he fell flat on his face. She ran into the kitchen. She heard a banging coming from the pantry, as she grabbed the rolling pin down that her grandmother always had hanging by the stove, but Mr Wolfe was upon her. She swung around and hit him across the head as hard as she could. He swayed, dazed by the attack. She brought the rolling pin up into his groin. He screamed and fell to the floor in agony.

Red ran over to the pantry and let her grandmother out. Grandmother took
the rolling pin while Red rang 000 for the police. Grandmother stood over Mr Wolfe. Every time he moved the rolling pin came down on a different part of his anatomy.

By the time the police arrived, Mr Wilbur Wolfe was more than happy to surrender himself to them. At his trial, he described Red and her Grandmother as 'demented' and 'in dire need of psychiatric help'. He was incarcerated for five years. When his time was almost up, he started a riot and received another three years for his efforts. He was a happy man

Is there anything else I should know?

I've made a mistake. How do I fix it?

On occasion you may find that you mark something incorrectly. If it is possible to use correction fluid without obscuring any other text or mark up, then this is the best solution.

If that is not possible then we use the 'stet' instruction. This means 'leave as original'. When the typesetter sees this, they ignore the instruction and take no action.

We place a broken line underneath the text that has been incorrectly marked, and the instruction 'stet' in the margin.

i.e. _ _ _ _ in the text and in  the margin.

What do I do if I have a question?

If you require to make a query about something then place a question mark in a circle against the area in question and add your question. Alternatively, use Post-it notes to convey your question.

A good way to highlight your question is to draw a box and place your question inside. This example is very simplistic, but you get the gist.

> **? Which is correct – Their or There?**

Example:

> As you can see colours mean different things to different people and cultures, at different times and in different contexts. Colors are all around us and they bring meaning to almost every facet of our lives.
>
> stet x2 / stet / ? spelling

Practical Proofreading

One last mini exercise. You accidentally mark the following incorrectly within the text:

1) Indicate a starting capital of *lady* in second line
2) Indicate a change to *Mother* in 2nd para 1st line.
3) Indicate an insert in *sideways* 2nd para 1st line.
4) Place a slash through the *comma* after *cold* in the last line.

You also have a question about the word 'curtsy' in the second last paragraph as you have never heard of a bus doing this before.

> 'Our children don't always understand when they are fortunate,' the old lady offered. She fiddled with her fur hat and adjusted her gloves, then rose stiffly to her feet.
>
> 'No, they don't,' said Mother, looking sideways at the old lady and wondered how she knew.
>
> 'Experience, my dear,' she said. 'My own daughter was not impressed when she had to live in England for four years. She was much the same age as your daughter. She will get over it.' She nodded towards Beverley.
>
> She turned to the bus as it pulled in beside them. Mother watched the bus 'curtsy' to allow the old lady to board with dignity and then followed her.
>
> She smiled as she followed Beverley to the back of the bus, as the so far cold, bleak day became suddenly warmer.

Major exercise 9

- Headings – First line – Bold, all caps, centred, blank line after,
- Sub- heading - bold, sentence case, centred. Blank line between heading and text.
- Paragraphs – First – full out to margin.
- Subsequent paras – indented, no blank line before.
- All 'flashback', 'flash-forward' – Italic, no initial caps unless required grammatically.
- Speech – single quotes.
- Excerpts – double quotes.
- Book titles - Italics.

Moving through Time
Flashbacks and Flash-forwards

In this paper I will endeavour to present the techniques of Flashbacks and Flash-forwards. I will also be looking at time travel in novels.

Flashbacks enable us to see into a character's past in real time and show, instead of tell, the details we need to know. A flash-forward gives us an inkling of what might happen in the future but it doesn't necessarily have to happen. Both devices can add depth to characters or suspense to the plot.
Flashbacks and   flash-forwards are useful devices but everything i could find on them, very firmly, advised they be kept to a minimum. The main plot, when using these devices, must stay in the novel's present time line. The flashback or **flash-forward** should, then, further this main plot and not just be a device the author wants to use for the sake of using it. It must provide information, emotion or add depth to the character or characters portrayed in the main plot in the present time.

A *flashback*, at the best of times, interrupts the flow of the main time line or plot so they should be kept short and meaningful.

Flashbacks can be presented as

1

memories.

Of course, entering the memory is fairly easy and there are several acceptable phrases to do this.

For example: "her memory suddenly went back to the day when..."; "this reminded him of the time...". There should then be a couple of uses of past perfect (had) to complete the transition

"As she rummaged through the drawer, she came across the necklice that had been a present from her husband. She remembered the sparkling day that he had given it to her. It had been a perfect time.

"The sun was high and hot. The picnic basket was crammed with delicious treats. It was a special day. They both knew it. Daryl spread the rug out under the shade of a large oak far enough away from the lake to make the view perfect...'

Continue your scene in real time using action and dialogue and then return to past perfect once or twice to show your reader that you are returning to the present. If necessary, another transition sentence can be used at this point. Exiting the memory must be achieved smoothly or else the time shift will appear stilted and will not work. It will annoy the reader and interrupt the flow of the story too much.

"Danielle had placed the necklace

around her neck so Daryl could admire it. But that wasn't possible anymore.

'Amy ran into the room. She was winging that Jake was teasing her. Danielle replaced her treasured necklace. She would have to wait for another time to finish her reminiscences. "Okay, Amy, let's go see if we can sort this out." She took Amy by the hand and they went in search of Jake."

Flashbacks can also take place in a dream or a state of unconsciousness. However, the rules still apply - they must be necessary to the main plot in present time, they must be short, and they must be entered and exited smoothly. Dialogue can also be used to contain a *flashback* or flash-forward, as can the general narrative.

Flash-forwards are less common than *flashbacks*, it seems. I have written a story using a type of flash-forward, but I don't believe I have read any books with any in them. My story involved a young mother running away from her responsibilities. She boards a train and heads off to a new life. On the train she meets a man and
they have a casual conversation. It turns out they are headed to the same town. When they arrive at the station, he gives her a lift and arranges some accommodation for her. She already has a job that she applied for before leaving. Over the next several months,

3

the two become close and spend time together but no romantic attachments are formed. She talks to him often of the family she left behind. He feels she has made a mistake so arranges for her husband and children to come on a surprise visit. When she sees them, she knows she has been a fool.

At the next train stop, she jumps up and leaves, thanking her companion for his company. It's un clear in the story whether she fell asleep and dreamt about the possible future or whether there was some magical intervention by the other passenger. And that's the way I wanted it.

Flash-forwards are probably most often used with psychic episodes, where someone either has the ability to see into the future or has an episode of doing so. With so much new Age thinking around nowadays, this is an acceptable way of persuading the reader to suspend their disbelief.

Another form of flash-forward is the foreshadowing. It easy is to use and effective when ending a scene or chapter.

For example, "Sam wished he could rid himself of the sick feeling in his gut that told him something terrible was going to happen, and happen soon."

As can be seen, it acts as a hook to keep the reader interested, dangling something that might be in front of the readers eyes. It does

4

not actually move the action into the future but in a way, moves the reader into the future, by having them wonder what is going to happen. It involves the reader and, therefor, is quite effective.

Various mechanisms such as the use of italics, a gap in the text, three asterisks are often used to shfit the time frame, and make them more evident to the reader, thus helping to prevent any confusion as to what is happening.

A more sophisticated form of *flashback* is called the 'time-shift'. It is more durable as a means to introduce a number of past experiences into the story. The types of phrases used to introduce the basic *flashback* are omitted.

To achieve this more subtle effect, you must concentrate on writing a seamless transition. This can be acheived by entering the consciousness of the POV character and by drawing the reader's attention away from the present scene with some generalisation, that causes the story to continue without being in a particular time. Then before the reader knows it, the story is taking place in a diffrent time.

There must a "novelistic present' where time occurs chronologically for *flashbacks* or *flash-forwards* to occur in any form. They must be able to exit and return to this time.

5

Flashbacks and *flash-forwards* should be avoided at times of high tension or critical stages in the story, as they will diffuse the excitement of the scenes.

Flashbacks are possibly most popular in romance and biographical novels, whereas *flash-forwards are* possibly used more in science fiction, and fantasy.

Before using the *flashback* and *flash-forward* techniques always consider whether the information needed can be, just as effectively or more effectively, delivered through dialogue or a brief though. If a *flashback* or *flash-forward* is seen to be the best way to show what is needed, they must make sense and further the present plot and they should be kept short so the plot in the present does not become stale.

Where this is probably mostly true, if we take such works as H. G. Well's *Time* Machine when the time Traveller returns from his

Some handy techniques

The following are some handy techniques to make your proofreading more accurate and easier.

- Before commencing to proofread, make sure you have made yourself familiar with any requirements, either through the Style Sheet or from direct instructions from your client/employer.

- Do a test proofread of a few pages to determine those elements that may be repetitive. This will help you to look out for these elements more easily and may make it quicker to complete the project.

- Use a bookmark or short ruler to guide your eye over the text. This makes reading much quicker and focuses the eyes so you can concentrate on turning off the auto-fix mechanism in your brain. It is natural for us to automatically fix small details we see to be the way they should be. We do it all the time and mostly are unaware that we are doing it. It is important, however, for a proofreader to switch this natural ability off during the proofreading process, otherwise we will miss the small errors that need to be corrected.

- Proofread headers and footers separately, checking the headers have the correct information and the footers also, especially page numbering. To do this, quickly scan the document checking the headers and then again to check the footers.

- Deliberately check any headings on each page, either by doing these first or by doing them as a separate action at the end of your general proofing, whichever seems the best method for the type of document.

- If a page has columns than treat each column as a page and use the gutter between the columns as a margin.

- Keep your marks as neat and compact as possible.

- Always print your letters; do not join them up.

- Never presume that a layout designer will know how to do something, especially such things as spelling. Always give clear, complete, and precise instructions.

- Take regular breaks. Proofread for only about an hour at a time then take a short break by doing something totally different. Avoid doing things like checking emails. Instead get up and move around – make yourself a cup of tea, go to the toilet, do a few minutes of exercise. This will keep you fit and alert.

- Initial or tick each page you complete as proof that you have proofread that page. At the end check that all pages have been initialled or ticked and that you have not missed any pages for any reason.

- If you need to ask a question of the author or editor, perhaps because you suspect that something is in error or needs further attention, you can use Post-it notes to explain what you need clarified rather than writing directly on the page. However, check what is acceptable first.

- If proofreading tables, you may find it easier to read down the columns as well as across. Any maths should be checked – addition, subtraction etc.

- Sometimes a book may be dead boring, or repetitive, or something you are just plain not interested in. If this is the case and you find your mind wandering, then try putting on some quiet music in the background. Having something else to do can help to focus your mind.

- A proofreader needs to know grammar, punctuation and spelling fairly well, or at least be able to detect when something is not right. Therefore, read – a lot. Also, invest in a good grammar reference and use whatever websites you find that 'speak' to you, in other words that explain things in a way that you can understand. We all think differently and so this is very important. There are many websites that have small quizzes for each subject, and these can be good to keep you in touch with what is correct.

- If working from home, come to some arrangement with those you live with that while you are working you will not be interrupted. It may take a few tries before you find something that works.

Check list

As a proofreader you need to look for the following types of problems and check the following aspects in the document you are proofreading.

- Spelling and punctuation errors.
- Layout errors.
    - Check that the same word does not end a line repeatedly.
    - Check that there are no blocks of white space (perhaps indicating some omission).
    - Check the font size and type.
    - Check the heading hierarchies are as per style guide.
- Word breaks – check that hyphenation is correct.
- Eliminate orphans and widows, if necessary.
- Any paragraph indentation is as per style guide.
- The spacing between lines, words and characters is correct.
- All preliminary pages are correctly included and numbered.
- Page numbers on all pages are as per style guide.
- Any lists are complete and logically kept together.
- All headings – running headers and footers, chapter headings, subheadings are on each page as specified.
- The Table of Contents reflects the correct headings and page numbers.
- Any List of Illustrations is accurate.
- Any captions are attached to the appropriate figures.
- Tables, diagrams, and figures. Check that these have been placed correctly within the document and are properly labelled.
- All end matter is complete, and pages numbered.
- The index is formatted as per style guide and is complete.
- All footnotes and references are complete.
- Mark where any material still needs to be included.
- Mark when any material has been repeated or deleted accidentally.
- Check that any previous corrections have been included.

Some handy references

Here are some reference books and websites you might find handy. The Style Manual and Macquarie dictionary are essentials.

1. *Style Manual for authors, editors and printers,* 6th Edition
   Published by John Wiley & Sons   ISBN 0-7016-3648-3
2. *Handbook for Writers and Editors,* by Margaret McKenzie
   Published by Dundas Press   ISBN 0-9578-6290-3
   The Australian Editing Handbook, by Elizabeth Flann and others
   Published by IDG Books   ISBN 1-7403-1088-8
3. *McGraw-Hill's Proofreading Handbook,* by Laura Anderson
   Published by McGraw-Hill   ISBN 0-0714-5764-X
4. *Macquarie Dictionary*
   Published by The Macquarie Library Pty Ltd
   (get a decent-sized one, at least the Essential version)
5. *Macquarie Thesaurus*
   Published by The Macquarie Library Pty Ltd

For an up-to-date Dictionary and Thesaurus, you could also subscribe to the *Macquarie Dictionary* and *Thesaurus* online at www.macquariedictionary.com.au

There are many good grammar websites available. Here I have included just a few you might find useful. I don't guarantee that they will still be around when you read this book but they were at the time of publication.

1. grammar.ccc.commnet.edu/grammar
2. www.dailygrammar.com
3. www.grammar.com
4. www.grammarly.com
5. www.stylemanual.gov.au

These books are useful grammar references.

1. *Grey Areas and Gremlins,* by Deb Doyle
   Available from the author, deb@hotlinks.net.au
   ISBN 0 646 42483 1
2. *Eats Shoots and Leaves,* by Lynne Truss
   Published by Profile Books Ltd.
   ISBN 1-8619-7612-7
3. *The Cambridge Guide to English Usage,* by Pam Peters
   Published by Cambridge Uni Press
   ISBN 0-5216-2181-X
4. *Troublesome Words,* By Bill Bryson
   Published by Penguin
   ISBN 0-1410-0135-1
5. *The Macquarie Writer's Friend: a guide to grammar and usage,*
   Published by The Macquarie Library Pty Ltd
   ISBN 1-8764-2909-7
6. *The Macquarie Speller's Friend*
   Published by The Macquarie Library Pty Ltd
   ISBN   1-8764-292-1

Quick Reference Mark-up Symbol Table

Mark-up symbol table

Change needed	Margin Mark	Mark in Text	Corrected copy
End of correction – required after EVERY margin instruction	/	None	n/a
Marked up incorrectly	stet/	-----	n/a
Inserting matter			
Change needed	Margin Mark	Mark in Text	Corrected copy
Insert character(s)	e/	This is th time	This is the time
Insert word(s) in text	the/	This is time	This is the time
Insert space(s)	#/ If more than 1 space is required add a 'times number' qualifier. e.g. # x 3/	This isthe time	This is the time
Insert blank line(s)	#/	This is the time for all good men	This is the time for all good men
Insert character as superscript formatted character	3/	This is the time	This is the time^2
Insert char as subscript formatted char	2/	This is HO	This is H$_2$O

Practical Proofreading

Replacing matter			
Change needed	**Margin Mark**	**Mark in Text**	**Corrected copy**
Replace character(s)	e/	This is th/ time	This is the time
Replace word(s) in text	is/	This are the time	This is the time
Deleting matter			
Change needed	**Margin Mark**	**Mark in Text**	**Corrected copy**
Delete a character in text	ℸ/	This is thee time	This is the time
Delete characters or word(s) in text	ℸ/	This is is the time	This is the time
Close up space between characters or words	⌒/	This i s the time	This is the time
Delete and close up text	ℸ̂/	This is thhe time	This is the time
Formatting paragraphs			
Change needed	**Margin Mark**	**Mark in Text**	**Corrected copy**
Begin a new paragraph	np/	This is the time for all to come to the party. The time is now.	This is the time for all to come to the party. The time is now.
New paragraph not required (run on)	r/o/ or run on/	This is ↩ the time	This is the time
Indent text from current position	⌐/	This is the time for everyone to rejoice.	This is the time for everyone to rejoice.
Start text at margin (delete indent) (full out)	fullout/ or f/o/	This is the time for everyone to rejoice.	This is the time for everyone to rejoice.

QUICK REFERENCE MARK-UP TABLE

Formatting text			
Change needed	**Margin Mark**	**Mark in Text**	**Corrected copy**
Change text to italic type	(ital)/	Underline text to be changed This is the time	This is *the time*
Change text to Roman type	(rom)/	Circle text to be changed This is *the time*	This is the time
Change text to bold type	(bold)/	Place wavy line under text to be changed This is the time	This is the **time**
Text needs to be underlined	(underline)/ or (u/l)/	Underline text to be changed This is the time	This is <u>the time</u>
Change text to capital letters	(caps)/ or (u/c)/	Place a triple underline under text to be capitalised e.g. this is the time	This is the time
Change text to lower case	(lc)/	TH̶I̶S̶ is the time	This is the time
Transpose (swap) characters or words	(trs)/	This is (time the)	This is the time
Centre text horizontally in line	(centre)/	⌐This is the time⌐	This is the time

115

Practical Proofreading

Punctuation			
Change needed	**Margin Mark**	**Mark in Text**	**Corrected copy**
Insert comma	,/	This is the time	This is the time,
Insert full stop	⊙/	This is the time	This is the time.
Insert colon	:/	This is the time	This is the time:
Insert semi colon	;/	This is the time	This is the time;
Insert question mark	?/	This is the time	This is the time?
Insert exclamation mark	!/	This is the time	This is the time!
Insert hyphen	=/	This is the two step	This is the two-step
Insert em-dash	⊢ᵐ⊣/ or ⊢em⊣/	This is the time	This is the time—
Insert en-dash	⊢ⁿ⊣/ or ⊢en⊣/	This is the time	This is the time–
Insert apostrophe	ʼ/	Its the time	It's the time
Insert single quotation marks	ʻ/ ... ʼ/	This is the time	This is the 'time'
Insert double quotation marks	"/ ... "/	This is the time	This is the "time"
Insert ellipsis	⋯/	This is the time	This is the time …
Insert solidus (slash)	//	This is was the time	This is/was the time
Move lines forward to next page (take over)	(t/o)	This is the time NP---------------- [for all good men	This is the time for all good men
Move lines back to previous page (take back)	(t/b)/	This is the time for all good men to come to the aid of NP---------------- the party.]	This is the time for all good men to come to the aid of the party.

116

Some more practice

to keep you going

Major exercise 10

- Title – bold, all capitals, centred. Blank line between headings and text.
- Sub-headings – 'n-dash Year nnnn n-dash – bold, full out to margin.
- Paragraphs – First – full out to margin.
- Subsequent paras – indented, no blank line before.
- Speech – single.
- *** at end of each time period – centred. Check these carefully.
- Page numbers – bottom, middle.

The Inevitable

– Year 2125 –

> <u>Notice to all</u> Regenerative <u>Cell Users</u>
>
> Due to a shortage of viable regenerative cell organisms, transplants will take place only in crucial cases. By order of the Council of Regenerative Cell Elders, until the current situation is relieved.
>
> This is believed to be a temporary problem.

'Jeez, Gary, will ya look at that? How in the hell could the government allow such a stupid thing to happen? Why, only last week I broke me arm hang-gliding. If it wasn't for regen cells I would have had to have my arm in plaster for weeks like they did in the old days. Bloody stupid, isn't it' Bob looked round at his best friend. At seventeen years old, they were both ambitious and opinionated, Bob intent on becoming a lawyer and Gary wanting to do bio-research.

'Yeah, did ya know that pre-regen, when people broke their backs they'd have to be in a chair with wheels 'cos they wouldn't be able to walk anymore. I'm sure glad we live now. Jeez, I musta broken me back at least five times now, Bob.

'And my old man, he told me people only used to live for about eighty years av. Gee, my dad's got socks older than that. Yeah, regen cells are sure the way to live. I'm glad it's 2125 and not 2000.

The two boys moved away from the noticeboard and continued on their way to school.

* * *

- Year 2162 -

'Your Honour, Mister Gary Mansfield has been in a coma now for six months. Prior to his accident he showed promise of becoming one of this nation's most brilliant biochemists. At fifty-four years of age he is still a young man with a great deal to offer this society. I put to you the necessity to release regen cells to aid in his recovery.'

'Mr Davies, your arguments will be considered, and this court will reconvene tomorrow at ten a.m.'

Bob sat down. The hearing had been the toughest of his career. His best friend was dying and there was nothing they could do. Nothing except to administer the extremely rare regen cell treatment. He thought back thirty-five years earlier to when everyone used regen cells as if donning a new jumper.

No one had realised that by using regen cells so extensively there would become a shortage and they would almost revert to pre-regen cell times. It had been horrible watching rich people take advantage of the system and poor people die because they couldn't afford to do anything else.

Then the authorities had introduced the hearings in order to assign the regen cells available in a more equitable way. At first it had seemed like an excellent solution but, law being law, clever, unscrupulous lawyers
would drain their clients of all their funds and leave them stranded and in worse condition than when they started. The hearings started taking months. In the meantime, sufferers would die. As each case came forward it took longer and longer.

Rob prayed that the decision returned would be a favourable one.

He remembered the night of Gary's accident Gary had rung him, sounding very excited about a breakthrough he had just made in his research. He had been on his way to show Bob his latest findings. It had piqued Bob's interest, for the first time in a long and jaded life. If Gary's accident had not occurred, all the misery and the hearings may not have been necessary, not only for Gary but for millions of others as well.

Now they were at the final stage and all Bob

could do was cross his fingers.

* * *

- Year 2220 -

'Hi, Gary, how's it goin'?' Bob felt thankful every time he heard Gary's voice.

'Not good, Bob. I'm glad you rang. I need your advice.' He went on to explain his dilemma.

'My God, man. They can't do that. First they develop regen cells and exploit them almost to extinction. Then once they've milked you dry in developing the artificial cell so there's plenty for everyone, they want you to develop a new strain. Who do they think they are? God? No, No, Gary. I cant just give you an answer over the phone. Come to my office, say in an hour? Okay, you see then.'

The line went dead.

Bob stood and went over to the window. The streets below were horribly crowded and even sixty floors up, through triple glazed windows, he could still hear the din of humanity below.

He picked up his binoculars and watched as a quarrel broke out amongst a couple of street vendors. They picked up their trolleys and rammed each other — once, twice. The third time both were thrown to the ground and their carts overturned. He could see mases of blood and was quite sure both were critically injured. In minutes an ambulance arrived and whisked them away. Bob knew that within the next hour or so both would be treated with regen cells to their damaged areas and with in days they would be back at their street stalls as if nothing had happened.

He saw this sort of thing all the time. No one respected life anymore.

He looked up the sky units being built. In the last fifty years every last inch of earth had been used. People now lived well into their second century and, in fact, it was believed, could almost live indefinitely.

Offshoots of regen cell technology had ensured an abundance of food for the ever-growing population.

He sighed and turned away from the depressing sight beyond his window. He knew what advice he he would give Gary when he arrived.

* * *

- Year 2243 –

Bob turned up his radio.

"There have been a record number of deaths reported in the city in the past week. An increase of nearly two ahd a half thousand percent. From a normal five to six deaths, mostly from the common cold, to a staggering fifteen thousand recorded deaths. The cause of these deaths is still under investigation. More on the late news.'

Gray had done the right thing. Bob had advised him to do as the government requested.

Bob looked across the coffee table at Gary. He looked old, all of his one hundred and eighteen years showed in his face, as he listened to the rest of the news. Bob watched as a tear trembled at the corner of Gary's eyes and finally toppled over the rim to trickle slowly down his cheeks. Life was cruel. Life without death was more so.

7

Major exercise 11

- Heading – bold, all capitals, centred. Two blank lines between heading and text.
- Paragraphs – First – full out to margin.
- Subsequent paras – indented, no blank line before.
- Speech – single quotes
- Page numbers – bottom, middle

THE CRYSTAL OF POWER

Dioptre looked around. Yesterday the village had been quiet. Now half the town was in panic, the other half in uproar. The Crystal of Power had been stolen during the darkest part of the night leaving the townspeople no longer under its protection, no longer encouraged to be trustworthy. Everyone knew who had perpetrated this unthinkable act. The Crystal must be returned to its tower, and returned quickly, or the whole country would be contaminated and evil would prevail. Dioptre hurried to her meeting with the king.

'Lady Dioptre, I request you're aid in this quest. Your talents are great. You may be our only hope,' insisted the King.

'But, Your Majesty, surely your army would be more suited to pursuing the thief of the crystal? I am but a woman with a few tricks up my sleeve.'

'Your "tricks" are more powerful than my whole army. Gudren must be stopped and it will take another witch to do it.'

Dioptre had her doubts that she alone could succeed, but she left the village that same afternoon on her griffin, Sepia.

'Come on, Sepia,' Dioptre urged, 'fly as if the wind would eat you if it caught you. We must reach Gudren's as quickly as we can.' They travelled quickly and far, making excellent time as the headed towards Gudren's keep.

On the edge of Gudren's domain the world tilted and Sepia fought to gain control as they plummeted. Gudren the evil witch, had shifted their dimension.

They plunged through the cloud cover and came to rest beside a road. They could hear singing coming out of a strange mist gathered before them.

Dioptre and Sepia felt bewildered by the magic worked on them and did not know what to make of the music.

Suddenly, a traveller stepped out of the mist.

'Do you require help, my Lady?' he inquired.

'Yes. Please tell me where we are?' said Dioptre, guardedly.

2

'Curious,' the traveller said under his breath. Out loud he said, 'You are in Acquitarius, my lady. I am *Prince* Myrrhdok, warlock, and your humble servant.' He bowed deeply. Her beauty enraptured him as it always enraptured those she met. This was one of her most useful powers.

'You are, perhaps, what is needed,' she mumbled. He looked at her questioningly. 'I am Dioptre, elf witch of Castella. I am on a quest demanding great urgency but I was caught in a trap and sent here. I must return immediately.'

'I will do all all in my power to help, my lady. Simply tell me what is needed and I will provide it.'

Both warlock and witch wore talismans to channel their powers. Each grasped hold of the other's talisman. dioptre spoke words of power. A portal formed before them, as she succeeded in breaking the strong spell that had sent them there.

'Thank you, my friend. My griffin and I must go now.' Dioptre and Sepia stepped through the portal. She gestured to close the gate, but at the last moment, Myrrhdok leapt through.

'You may need my help again, my lady,' he said and

3

strode off. For a moment Dioptre and Sepia stood and watched the strange warlock walk off into the distance and then they followed him.

They travelled swiftly and encountered no further traps, and arrived at the foot of Gudren's keep in no time. The evil witch,s pet dragon, Petard, guarded the entrance. They could see the glow of the Crystal of Power high in the tower above.

"This dragon is a fierce one,' said Myrrhdok. 'If you can free the crystal, I will solve the problem of the dragon.' Dioptre nodded. With a small, graceful gesture Sepia and Dioptre vanished leaving only a faint breeze behind them.

Myrrhdok stepped out. He tossed an insubstantial ball of mist from one hand to the other, and whistled a cheery tune.

'Who goes there?' bellowed the ugly dragon.

'Only Myrrhdok, the magician, come to show you a trick.'

'Do not come closer.'

Myrrhdok stopped. He was close enough.

* * *

4

Practical Proofreading

Dioptre and Sepia flew swiftly to the top of the tower. There were no other guards there. Obviously, Gudren had ultimate faith in her dragon.

'Stay here,' she commanded Sepia and climbed off the griffin's back.

The tower surrounding the crystal shimmered with the evil being fed to the ball. Dioptre took down the crystal from its clawed stand. It felt heavy with evil. She fought the **suffocating** atmosphere as return to Sepia so they could fly to safety. Sepia tried to help her mistress to climb back onto her back, but she was badly feeling the effects of the evil. Dioptre, too, felt the effects of the evil seeping from the tower. She drew on the last of her power to weave a spell of clarity and protection around them. Then she flung herself upon Sepia's back and encouraged the griffin to lift into the air.

Sepia's wings beat more slowly each second they stayed on the tower. With an enormous effort she directed all the strength she could muster into lifting her wings and her body from the tower top. She hoped her strength would last long enough for them to reach safety beyond Gudren's reach. Sepia flew shakily away from the tower.

Gudren saw them flying away and knew immediately that her evil plan had failed. She screamed, enraged that they should be so bold. She flung bolts of lightning at them but Sepia was out of range.

Myrrhdok saw the griffin limping away and threw his mist at the dragon's eyes. It was not strong enough to kill it but it would confuse it. He turned and fled, as the evil witch began to scream.

the evil gradually seeped from the crystal as Dioptre and Sepia flew further and further away from Gudren's keep. When they deemed it safe, they landed to rest. Within minutes, Myrrhdok had joined them.

On the journey home, they exchanged stories of their relevant tasks. Dioptre amazed at Myrrhdok's courage in the face of an angry dragon.

Myrrhdok wondered what was to happen now. Dioptre was far too fascinating to leave behind and return to his own home. For now, though, he would just enjoy their journey back to Castella.

Gudren made one last attempt to resecure the crystal, when they were only a day away from the CRYSTAL Chamber. She ordered Petard to attack them. But Dioptre and Myrrhdok proved too strong. Together they summoned an earth spring and sent it into the air.

The terrified Petard panicked and Gudren fell from its back, saving herself at the last moment by digging her claw-like nails into one of its wings. Petard turned and fled. He was not about to continue fighting when he knew he could not win.

Dioptre, Myrrhdok and Sepia laughed at the sight of Gudren desperately clinging to the dragon's wing, screaming worse and worse obscenities at him, which he completely ignored. They were sure it would be quite some time before Gudren would be a problem again.

Two days had passed since the crystal was taken. There had been much destruction in that short time. Dioptre set the crystal in its rightful place in the Crystal Chamber. Almost immediately the people of Castella became the people she knew and loved again. The Crystal of Power was returned'.

7

Major exercise 12

- Headings – Title page – bold, all capitals, no page number, centred, Chapters – bold, sentence case, centred, chapter number spelled out. Blank line between headings and text.
- Paragraphs – First – full out to margin.
- Subsequent paras – indented, no blank line before.
- Speech – single quotes.
- Dragon name – Garenthal.

Sir Henry and the Dragon

Chapter One

The two young knights fought valiantly, each a perfect match for the other. Wooden sword clashed on wooden sword. Henry blocked Tom, only to be blocked in turn. They fought back and forth, up and down the yard. Hours seemed to pass, but still they fought on neither willing to give in to the other. Even when Henry's mum called them in for a drink and a snack, they kept on fighting, trying to outwit each other. But it was no good. They were to well matched. In the end they both collapsed on the grass, gasping for breath and exhausted, mutual in their agreement that their fight was a draw.

Henry closed his eyes against the sun still beaming strongly down onto them. His mind started to drift. He could hear Tom beside him, tapping his feet on the ground, could hear the birds calling in the trees as it grew closer to sundown and he could hear the creak of the clothesline as it turned lazily in the slight breeze.

A large shadow passed overhead. He could see it through his closed eyelids. He thought it must be a cloud. He hoped it wasn't going to rain. Then realised the sounds around him were different. There was no creeking clothesline. Instead there was the sound of wind whipping through trees. Tom's tapping feet changed into the sound of pounding hooves and the birdsong changed to enraged screams.

Henry opened his eyes and jumped to his feet. Coming straight for him was a blood red dragon. He grabbed the sword from the ground at his feet and dodged the sharp talons just in time.

Chapter 2

'Run, Sir Henry,' called a knight on the back of a huge armoured horse. Henry was still confused but all his instincts came to his rescue. The hours he had spent playing games on his computer meant that he had lightning quick reflexes and his mind was used to the extraordinary happening. When he had Tome he would sit down and work out what on earth was gong on. But now he thought he had to find somewhere safe to hide.

Henry turned towards the forest and ran as fast as his armour-clad body could take him. He was, perhaps, not known for his speed, generally fear and need spurred him on faster than normal.

He knew from his computer games that zigzagging and mazes were wonderful diversions. He was still out in the open so zigzagging was the best thing for the moment but once inside the forest he would weave his way through the trees in a maze of a path that would make it difficult for the dragon to follow him.

As he ran, dodging first left and then right, forcing the dragon to continually shift its weight and swerve to follow him, Henry could hear the shouts of other knights around him. There were perhaps three or four others all trying to attract the dragon's attention away from Henry so he could escape but they were not having any success. The dragon was fixed on Henry and nothing was going to sway it from its course.

Henry turned his head and took a quick look over his shoulder. The dragon was gaining on him. Henry waved his sword and shouted, 'You don't want to come near me. I'm good with this.' The next thing a bright yellow flame shot from the dragon's nostrils and Henry watched in dismay as his sword burst into flames. He dropped the flaming sword, turned and fled towards the forest.

Chapter 3

The dragon overtook him and landed just before the trees. He spread out his wings to prevent Henry from continuing. 'Your kind is not permitted here,' it bellowed. 'The forest belongs to the dragons.'

'Rubbish,' shouted Henry. 'The forest belongs to everyone. Anyway, the only reason we're here is because you are so nasty. Chasing us down and burning our swords and frightening everyone. That's why all these knights are hunting you, you know.'

'Go, or I will burn you up.' The dragon stared into Henry's eyes. Henry stared back. Suddenly Henry was not afraid. There was something else going on here.

'I don't believe you. You'll burn me as soon as I move.' Henry stepped cautiously to his right. The dragon followed, preventing him from going further. Spears shot past Henry. One pierced the right wing of the dragon and made him howl. Other spears followed. Henry turned and found an army bearing down on them. The three knights, who had been trying to distract the dragon before, streaked past, yelling for Henry to run. The dragon took to the skies again and Henry ran on into the safety of the forest.

He ran on and on until he was deep into the forest.
Finally he had to stop to rest. He came upon a huge

stack of tumbled boulders. When he searched for a safe place to sit he came across an opening to a cave. 'Just the thing,' he thought, and went through the opening. He stopped just inside to let his eyes get used to the dim light. It was enormous. He couldn't see the back of the cave at all and the sides were just dim shadows on the left and right of him. Henry moved in further. He tripped over something. It was a shield held in the tight grip of an armour-clad skeletalarm. He backed away from it, terrified at the gruesome sight. He moved further in and found more evidence of gruesome deeds. It began to occur to him that maybe the cave wasn't the safest place to be after all.

Chapter 4

Henry kept wandering deeper into the cave. The light stayed at a soft dim glow and the temperature a warm summer's day warmth. It was odd; you would expect it to grow darker and colder the further you went into a cave. This was definitely not good!

Henry slowed his steps. He could sense something up ahead. It came up to about his waist level and was about his arms outstretched wide. As he drew closer he could see that there was a light cover over the top of the container. The container was rough and seemed to be made from branches and twigs and mosses. It looked a little like a nest. Carefully he lifted the cover and peeked underneath. Nestled in the centre of the nest were three orange eggs. 'Oh, no, this must be what he was worried about,' said Henry out loud.

'Yes and now you must die.' While Henry had been exploring cave the the dragon had crept in quietly behind him.

Chapter 5

Henry sprang around to face the huge creature. "I will not harm your eggs,' said Henry trying to sound calm but in fact feeling like his legs were going to give way at any moment.

'You will not have the chance,' spoke the dragon carefully. The human language was not natural to the dragon. It was obviously an effort for him to form the words so Henry might understand. As it was, Henry had to listen carefully to hear the words between the growls and the hisses that came from the dragon's enormous mouth.

'I do not want to harm any humans,' said the dragon. 'I just want to be left in piece to raise my children. We are the last of our kind now. I will go away with my young once they are hatched and find a place where no man will walk. But I must be given Tome for my eggs to hatch.'

'What happened to your wife.' asked Henry realising that it was normally the female dragon's duty to watch over the eggs.

A huge sorrowful sigh blew out from the dragon's nostrils. 'She was out hunting for food but the knights came and slaughtered her. Our eggs were only newly hatched but able to be left for short periods of Tome. I have had to work hard to keep them alive since Medora was slain.'

'I should introduce myself,' said Henry. 'My

10

name is Henry.'

'I am Garanthal,' said the Dragon. 'You do not speak the way other humans speak. Why is that?'

'Um – actually if we are going to talk, would you mind lying down? My neck is getting sore.'

Garenthal was only too willing to oblige. There was something more here than met the eye. Garenthla wondered, even hoped, that he might find a solution to his problems.

Chapter Six

'I'm not really sure what happened, but I was playing at sword fighting with my friend Tom. We were pretending to be knights, mighty knights, but neither of us could gain on advantage over the other. After playing for hours, at least, we agreed that the game was a draw. We lay down on the grass and I closed my eyes from the sun. The next thing I knew I was here, dressed like this and you were flying overhead. Dragons don't really exist where I come from, although we have lots of stories about them but no one has ever really seen one or found any remains either. Strange, hey?'

He looked up into the dragon's great face. Garenthal's fiery eyes were thoughtful and perhaps just a little confused.

'You say there are no dragons in your land?'
Henry nodded.
'And you don't know how you came to be here?'
Henry shoook his head this time.
'Well, Sir Henry, I think I might be able to return you to your Tome and place. I didn't really want to kill you and as you won't be a threat once you go back I won't need to.

'I believe you may have passed through a doorway. There are a few in this land but not many know of them. I, however, know of one that you will be able to use. It is right here in this cave.'

12

'So — what do I have to do?' asked Henry, a little sad that he would have to leave this land of dragons, but he knew he needed to return.

'First, you need to think very strongly about your home. Have you got a strong image?' Henry nodded. He had closed his eyes to help him see it properly. The dragon moved closer and scooped up his eggs, depositing him in a sack beneath his wing. 'Now wish with all your heart that you were home and take an slow step forward."

13

Chapter Seven

'Yeah, I think we should play something on the computer now. How about that new game Jason got for you? You know that one about dragons.' Tom shoved another piece of biscuit in his mouth.

Henry looked around. He was back home as if nothing had happened.

'What do you say?' Tom repeated.

'Yeah, okay.'

Henry heard a scratching sound outside the back window. He looked out to see a puff of smoke behind the carport. He was just about to yell fire when he spotted a huge eye winking at him through the gap.

'I'll be back in a minute, Tom. I left something outside. Go in and start up the computer.' He raced out the back door and up the yard.

'Garenthal, is that you? Is that really you?' he almost shouted.

'Ssh, Henry. Of course, it's me. Do you know any other dragons?'

'No, I mean, I thought it was all a dream or something. I didn't think you were real,' he whispered loudly.

'We are and thank you for the lift to your home land. Now we will be safe from hunters. As soon as it is dark we will leave and find a nice barren place that no one will find us in.' A little whimper sounded underneath Garenthal's wing.

'Is that ...?' asked Henry.

14

'Yes, meet Dorian, Wildemere and Trance. They hatched as we passed through the portal.'

'I'll miss you, Garenthal,' said Henry. 'Can't you stay around so we can visit each other'

'I'm afraid not, Henry. Your world is probably no safer than mine, especially as you say you have stories of dragons but no evidence. That probably means dragons were hunted to extinction many thousands of years ago. I need to keep my family safe and to do that I need to disappear.'

Henry nodded.

Tom suddenly called out the back door.

'Ill be right there, Tom,' Henry called back.

'I hope I'll see you again some Tome,' said Henry.

'I hope so too,' said Garenthal. 'Perhaps when you're grown you'll remember me and come looking for my barren place. I'll make sure I leave markers. You'll understand them if you come looking.' Garenthal laid the tip of his wing on Henry's head. Henry felt a slight shock race

through him that left him feeling warm. He knew that Garenthal had left him with the knowledge to find the dragons when the Tome came.

He leant over and hugged the dragon as best he could, considering their hugely different sizes and then he gave him one last look and went inside to join Tom.

'What are you grinning about?' asked Tom.

15

Practical Proofreading

'Oh, nothing. Nothing at all,' said Henry and not for the world would he ever tell anyone of his afternoon's adventure.

Solutions to Exercises

Solutions to Exercises

Page 25 Replacing characters

> What makes a stary? Good questun, you say, what does make a story?
>
> A story occurs when a protjonixt (hero) is taken out of their normal rootine world and given a problem to solve, a goal to achieve. In solving this problem they undergo change and groe and at the end of the story are different to what they were at the beginning. They experiance conflicts from external and internal influances (conflicts here being obstacles in their way). There is generally an antagonist – someone or something – that puts the externtl barriers in their way, often with the same, but opposing goal, as the hero.

Page 29 Inserting words and characters

> ### OUR SECRET LOVE
>
> We shared a secret love, full furtive looks, fleting hand touches, and not walking home opposite direction.

Page 31 Inserting spaces and punctuation

> No one knew but us. Itwas difficult but delicious, too Our little secret, punctuated with beating hearts anda longing deep enough to giveme cramps every time our eyes met. Like now.
>
> "Oh, get a room you two" chorused the class. We both blushed Maybe our secret love was notso secret afterall.

151

Practical Proofreading

Page 32 Inserting dashes

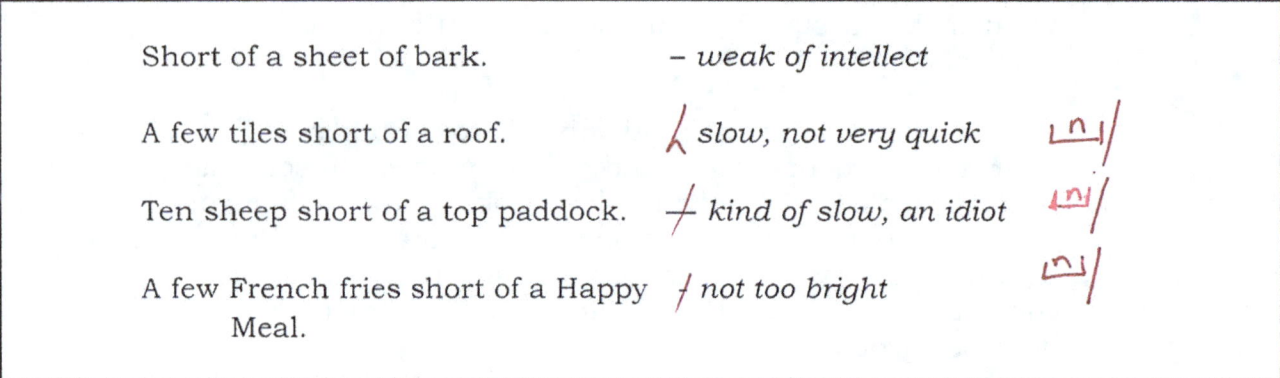

Page 34 Inserting apostrophes and quotes

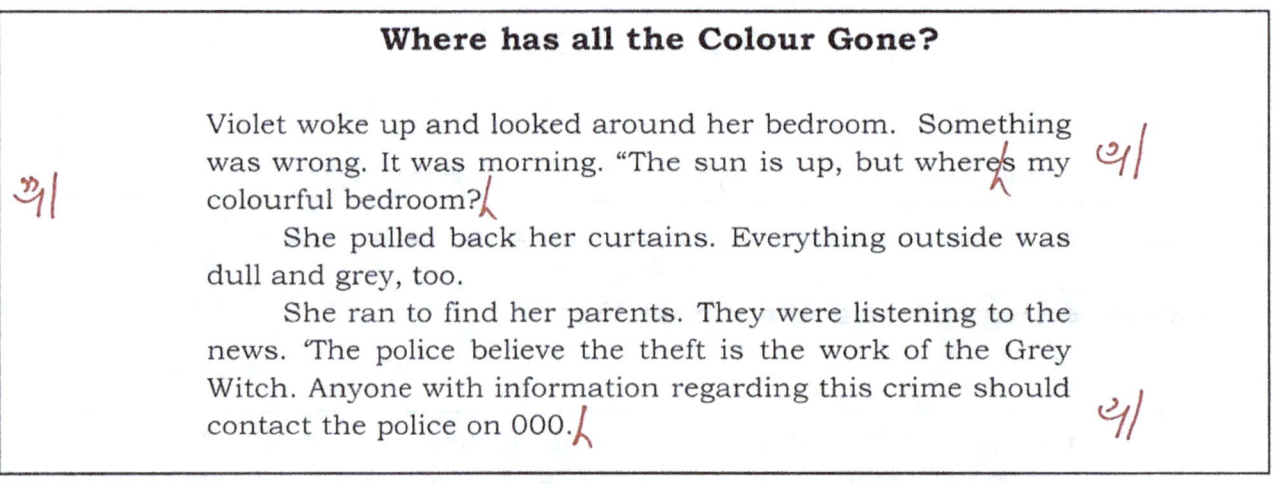

Page 35 Specifying Superscript

'The Egyptians used lapis lazuli to represent Heaven.'

_____

1 www.crystal-cure.com, Amerindea Crystal-cure, Color meaning, 2004.

Solutions to Exercises

Page 35 Specifying subscript

> Similarly, subscripts are also used frequently in mathematics to define different versions of the same variable: for example, in an equation x_0 and x_f might indicate the initial and final value of x, while v_{rocket} and $v_{observer}$ would stand for the velocities of a rocket and an observer. Commonly, variables with a zero in the subscript are referred to as the variable name followed by "nought" (e.g. v_0 would be read, "v-nought").

Page 36 Extra Subscript and Superscript practice

> What is the cube of 30? i.e. 30^3
>
> Answer: 27,000
>
> The backyard is $5m^2$.
>
> The formulas for the following are:
>
> Hydrogen peroxide—H_2O_2
> Hydrogen—H_2
> Dichlorine Hexoxide—Cl_2O_6

Page 36 Inserting Spaces

> Every book must have a problem to solve, or goal to achieve, whether it is a stand-alone book or part of a series. The protagonist must change from the start of the book to the end of the book, for the better, preferably. This occurs through the conflicts the protagonist encounters, learns from and defeats.

Practical Proofreading

Page 40 Inserting indents, new paragraph and blank lines

'I don't know what we'll do,' said Mum. 'The Rainbow Wizard was the only one who could fix it before, but he's gone.'
Violet started to cry.

Mum and Dad hugged her. 'It's all right,' said Dad. 'The colours will come back.' Violet's day was awful. No one could concentrate without colours. The teachers were grouchy, and the children were naughty

Page 47 Deleting characters and words

She raced home when school was finished too find out if the Grey Witch had been caught, but she hadn't been. They really needed the Rainbow Wizard.
She thought and thought until she had an idea. Her computer would help save the world!
The chat room buzzed. She typed in her message. 'Rainbow Wizard only hope. Everyone look for him him.' Her screen started flickering with questions, but Violet had no answers.
Then shee remembered what her parents had told here. 'He's probably the only only colour left. Keep your eyes open.'

Page 49 Deleting spaces and blank lines

Children all over the world began looking for the Rainbow Wizard. They searched the forests, the mountains,

and all the buildings. They went into the sewers, looked behind every door and checked the oceans. But no one found him.
Violet al most gave up hope. She lay down on the grass to think and looked up at the white clouds. A patch of rainbow winked at her. She blin ked. It did it again.

She jumped to her feet and shouted, 'Rain bow Wizard we need you. Please come down.'

Solutions to Exercises

Page 50 Run on

The Rainbow Wizard left his safe cloud and joined Violet on the ground.
'You have to fix the colours.'
The Wizard shook his head.
'Why not?' asked Violet.
'Last time it made me go grey and dull. It took me ages to get my colour back.'
'But all this grey is making people go crazy. I'll help you find the Grey Witch and stop her for good.'

Page 51 Full out

The wizard thought for a second.

'Okay.' He spread his arms and turned around slowly. The colours started coming back. By the time his circle was complete the wizard had lost all of his rainbow colouring.

With help from the chat room, they found the Grey Witch in a cave in the Black Mountains. The Rainbow Wizard cast a spell on her so she would never be able to steal colour again.

The Wizard and Violet became good friends. Gradually his colours came back. Due to Violet's quick thinking no one would have to worry about colour being stolen again.

Page 67 TRS

'Will stop you that?' said her mother. 'It's very annoying, and it won't make the bus get here any quicker.' She her pulled gloves on tighter and hunkered into her thick coat.

155

Practical Proofreading

Page 69 Take over and take back

[Beverley stopped tapping her feet and stood up
New page--
instead to give her seat to an elderly woman who just joined them.

   Beverley began to pace up and down. She dug her hands into her pockets and went backwards and forwards. Her mother glanced heavenwards willing for the bus to turn up soon.

   The elderly woman sighed as she sat
New page--
 down. 'Was clocken det buss?' she asked.]

Page 85 Changing text to capitals

    mother looked at her blankly. 'I'm sorry but i don't speak swedish,' she said, wringing her gloved hands together and, not for the first time, wishing she had taken the time to take some lessons.

Page 86 Changing text to lower case

    'You are English?' the elderly Lady said, her accent thick.

   'No. No, Australian,' saiD Mother.

Page 86 Specifying Italic text

   'Mum when is the bus coming? I'm sick of sitting out here in the cold. Why couldn't we have got here closer to the time?' Beverley glared at her mother. 'I don't know why we couldn't have a car here. Public transport is so gay. It takes forever to get anywhere.'

Solutions to Exercises

Page 87 Specifying Roman text

(rom)/ 'Dear, the bus is only (about) five minutes away now. (rom)/
Then we'll be able to get on our way. You know they changed
the timetable on us; otherwise we would have been on the bus
already. And you know that we decided it was (cheaper) for us (rom)/
(rom)/ to (forget) about a car while we were here and safer, too,
(rom)/ considering we know (nothing) about driving in the snow.'
(rom)/ Mother's (face) had turned bright red.

Page 88 Specifying bold and unbold text

(unbold)/ The **elderly** lady ignored her reaction to Beverley's
rudeness. Instead she continued as if they had not been
interrupted, her original question having already been
answered.

(bold)/ 'Are you here on holiday?' the old **lady** asked, in her (unbold)/
heavily accented but almost perfect English.

Page 89 Specifying underlined text

(u/L)/ 'No, my husband works for <u>Ericsson's</u>. He has a contract (u/L)/
here.' <u>Mother</u> spoke slowly and clearly. It was always difficult
to know how much English people knew but she could always
count on it being more than the Swedish she knew.

'How long will you be here?' the old <u>lady</u> continued. She (u/L)/
(u/L)/ smiled warmly at <u>Mother</u>, ignoring <u>Beverley</u> completely. (u/L)/

Page 89 Centre text

(centre)/ [The Bus Stop]

The bus was still fifteen minutes away. Beverley tapped her
feet and gazed around.

157

Practical Proofreading

Page 90 Aligning text

'About two years, we think.' She shifted on her seat and looked up the road in the direction of the bus.

'That is a great adventure,' said the old lady.

'Yes. Tell Beverley that,' muttered Mother.

Page 100 Others

'Our children don't always understand when they are fortunate,' the old lady offered. She fiddled with her fur hat and adjusted her gloves, then rose stiffly to her feet.

 'No, they don't,' said Mother, looking sideways at the old lady and wondered how she knew.

'Experience, my dear,' she said. 'My own daughter was not impressed when she had to live in England for four years. She was much the same age as your daughter. She will get over it.' She nodded towards Beverley.

She turned to the bus as it pulled in beside them. Mother watched the bus 'curtsy' to allow the old lady to board with 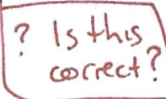 dignity and then followed her.

 She smiled as she followed Beverley to the back of the bus, as the so far cold, bleak day became suddenly warmer.

Solutions to Major Exercises

Major 1 page 41

HOMELESS

He was tired, tired and hungry. He sat down on the cold concrete, his back against the lamppost.

People rushed past him. He wondered where they were all going in such a hurry. The traffic behind him was deafening with the honking of horns, the revving of engines.

Few people noticed the man sitting quietly on the ground as they rushed past. Those did looked at his dirty clothes and sunken face with distaste. No one understood.

The man watched the clocks above the station entrance. His eyes focused on the one telling the current time. He watched the second hand move precisely around the face. As he watched, the people and cars disappeared. There was only the clock — the second hand and ticking he could so clearly hear.

The ticking matched the beating of his heart. The hands kept travelling unrelentingly around the clock face.

1

Practical Proofreading

Suddenly they stopped. There was no longer any sounds, no longer rushing people and impatient cars.

At two a.m. the ambulence officers loaded his stiff cold body into the back of their ambulance. Another John Doe was added their list

Major 2 Page 43

A Big Lady with a Big Heart

Her voice is touched with a light Kiwi accent. She was born under the star sign Sagittarius on 12th December 1959, in Murupara, not far from Rotorua, New Zealand. She describes herself as 'big, brave, determined, relentless, passionate, lovable, honest and seeking'. She is sentimental, and her favourite film is *The Sound of Music*. She dotes on her family, and enjoys spending time talking with her children, Emma – fifteen, and Catherine – seven. Her adored husband is Ben, aged forty-six. She has two brothers, one of which she is close to; the other was always mean to her. She loves *Dr Phil* and *Oprah*. Her favourite book is *Jonathan Livingston Seagull* which 'expanded her wings, allowing her to explore life outside her own little box'. She has now spent more time in Australia than in New Zealand. She migrated twenty-four years ago and is an Australian citizen, because she wanted to be able to vote, something she had never been able to do in her own country. She lives in South Morang but would prefer a more open country abode.

Her name is Patricia.

In order to give her children good choices in their lives Patricia is striving to provide them with good educations, something she missed out on herself. She says that Emma 'tries to mother her and is her reality check', whereas, Catherine is 'dynamic, wild, a cat with an enormous personality who takes risks'.

Patricia's life is bound up in her family, leaving her limited spare time to pursue hobbies. In a typical display of her quirky sense of humour, some of her 'hobbies' include: cleaning the kitty litter tray, cuddling her cat, putting clothes on the line and ironing. If given her druthers, however, Patricia would lie in bed, reading one of her favourite books. Patricia is full of stories. Like the one when the family decided they would like to try the fish and chips at Rex Hunt's D'lish Fish. They were not exactly sure where it was located. Patricia insisted it was in St. Kilda. Her husband insisted it was in Port Melbourne. They drove around for a while and failed to find it. So they pulled into a service station to ask for directions. Before Ben could get out of the car, another vehicle pulled up beside them. Rex Hunt climbed out. They chatted to him for a while and were directed to Port Melbourne.

Patricia says she 'wouldn't change anything about herself and is happy with where she is'. This is an enormous achievement.

On top of this she is pursuing a dream; a dream to write, exploring what she likes and what she does well. Like so many others she has begun the Diploma in Professional Writing and Editing. Good Luck, Patricia!

Major 3 Page 52

Poets' Breakfast 26 June 2004
Kilmore Celtic Festival

A friend and I attended the annual Poets' Breakfast at the Kilmore Celtic Festival held on 26th June 2004 in the Kilmore Scout Hall, Kilmore.

This was the fifth Poets' Breakfast to be held. They were started by Phil Clancy who M.C.s the proceedings. He wanted to foster local interest and talent in poetry, although he does not write poetry himself.

There are two parts to the Breakfast: readings of poet's own poetry for the Sid Cantlon Poet's Award sponsored by the Kilmore Mechanics Institute; and, basically, an open reading section where anyone can read their own or other people's poetry.

The Trophy is an interesting one. It is made from an old fence post and part of it has been left rough while part has been polished, symbolising the process of the rough poem to the polished poem or poet. The winner of each year is engraved on brass plates attached to the main trophy and they also receive a small round polished piece of local blackwood with a brass engraved plaque. This they can keep as a happy reminder of their success.

Sid Cantlon was a local drover who worked all over Australia. He was also a poet who wrote many poems about local Kilmore identities and the area itself. He lived in a tent and loved the life.

It costs $10.00 to attend the Breakfast or you can buy a Day ticket to the Festival, at $30.00, which gains you entry to other Celtic events on the day. The $10.00 entitles you to a seat at the Breakfast. If you wish to eat, you must pay for whatever you order. Prices are reasonable and you get a nicely laid out table with white tablecloths and comfortable chairs to eat at. It is really quite well presented.

Phil Clancy kicked off the proceedings wiyh reading and then the competition entrants had their say. There were ten entrants, including my friend and me. They were all ages from teens to people in their seventies and equal numbers of men and women. There was a policeman, a lady who had never read or written anything before who was reading her first poem, to poems that were written on the spot. You could tell everyone was passionate about poetry and truly enjoyed writing and reading their poetry to other people.

At the end of the competition section, each member of the audience was handed a strip of paper and asked to vote on the poet they thought was best.

While the votes being counted, people came forward and read poems written by other people, some of them written by locals who were too shy to get up themselves to poems by C. J. Dennis and Banjo Patterson. My friend and I read another poem in this section as well.

On the whole, the poetry read was mainly in a ballad style and most were about the local Kilmore area, local notable residents or personal experiences. Rhyming poems were by far the most favoured. In fact, I think there was only one poem that didn't rhyme.

Finally, the time came to find out who was to be this year's Syd Cantlon Poet's Award winner. Previous years had seen, in 2000 Don Austin; 2001 Jason

Sedgewick; 2002 and 2003 Uma Brown, take home the trophy. All three had read poems this year. After a slight drum roll, Uma Brown was announced as the winner for the third year in a row.

Assumption College Kilmore were kind enough to provide gas heaters to heat the hall and the Kilmore Scout group provided breakfast and th hall to have it in.
Next year they are considering having a Poets' Supper instead as some people are finding it hard to get to the breakfast early on the cold winter mornings. However, other activities in the Celtic Festival would then be be competing with it and it might mean some people would opt to attend some other event instead of the Poets Supper.
Since the Breakfast started, the organisers have taped the readings with a view that, one day, they would like to produce an anthology. As my husband typeset and designed my Writers Group anthology, he and I have offered to to produce an anthology this year. It woud be great if this could be an ongoing feature of the Breakfast.
All in all, it is a very fun way of enjoying poetry readings. The downside being that it happens only once a year. My friend and I will return next year, having spent some, if not all, of the next twelve months perfecting our ballad style.

Major 4 Page 55

THE SPECIAL BOND

I have a memory; a vague notion, of kind, sad face gasing at me over the edge of my cot. I can still feel the love and closeness in that simple acct.

I was only a month old at the time; my sister was five and my brother almost eight.

At four years old I realised Dad was missing and I tried to find out why.

'Mum why don't I have a dad like everyone else?' I looked at her, willing her to give me the answer I wanted.

My mothers face remained impassive as if to talk about my dad was to open a door she had locked long ago and forgottten where she had put the key. Mistiness clouded her eyes. 'I'm sorry, sweetie, but Daddy went away a long time ago.'

'Will he come back soon.'

'No, love, he won't.' She turned back to pealing the potatoes. 'Now go and play with your sister, like a good girl. I have to get tea ready now.' She lifted a hand to brush at the tears that threatened to fall.

Tears welled in my eyes, too, as I watched her. I could feel the grief rise from her in waves and I felt terrible that I had made her so sad.

[closeup]

From that time onwards I listened closely and remembered everything I heard about my father. I asked my brother and sister what they remembered, and aunties and uncles, too. And then I reached inside myself and found the rest of him.

Whenever I was troubled, I would call on him to help me. And he would come.

Somehow in that last moment of his life, when he peered at me over my cot, he created a bond between us that survived even death. When I talked to him I could see him, touch him and hear him. He was real. But only to me. And he was everything, and more, that I could ever have wished for in a father.

'I wish Emma would play with me, Dad. But she's always too busy doing her "grown up" things. She's only five years older than me. She's not grown up at all,' I pouted.

Dad was silent for a minute. 'It won't be long before you will understand what she means. Just wait a short time. I promise it will all be okay.'

'But that doesn't help me. She's such a snob!'

'Who are you calling a snob? And who are you talking to?' Emma poked her head into my room, a look of disgust on her face. 'Oh, you're not talking to "Dad" again, are you?' she taunted. She had never been able to see Dad. I think it made her angry to know that I could do something she couldn't.

'Yes, I'm talking to Dad and don't you dare say he isn't here. Because I know he is.' I jumped up, ready to defend myself.

'Oh, come off it, Joanie. You know it's all your imagination. Grow up or something. Or do you *want* to end up at the nut farm?'

'Don't you dare call me crazy? I'm not.' I flew at her, all my rage seeming to explode at once.

'Joan — stop!' Dad said so quietly I nearly didn't hear him. There was authority in his voice, and disapproval. I had never heard that there before. I stopped dead in my tracks.

'Let it be,' he continued now that he had my attention. 'You know I am here only for you. You can't blame Emma for not believing.'

'But she should, Dad, she should!' I insisted. I looked at Emma. She rolled her eyes. 'Well, you should!' I said to her.

'Nuts! Definitely nuts!' she muttered and fled to her own room.

'You really shouldn't do that, you know,' said Dad.

'Why? She's always so *superior*. If she only *believed*, maybe she'd be able to hear you and see you, too.'

'No, she wouldn't because *she* doesn't need me, but you do.'

I thought about that for a minute and when I looked up at Dad again, he was gone. He always did that, gave me something to think about and time to think about it.

He was always there for me. I could tell him anything. And I asked him about everything, too. He would explain things so I could understand. It was great! We both had the same sense of humour and we would spend hours laughing at each other's jokes.

But then it all fell apart.

When I was eighteen I met someone special. He was warm and sweet and considerate and I liked him a lot. I was a little nervous about telling Dad but in the end I told him all about him. Everything except that my special man was married.

Our first date was a wonderful evening. We drove down to the beach and walked along the shoreline, talking. After a while we grew tired and sat down to gaze out past the breakers, our hands entwined. For the first time that evening we were silent, but it was a comfortable silence, no awkwardness at all. Gradually we crept closer and, finally, we kissed. When he pulled reluctantly away, my breath was coming in short gasps. But I wanted more, so I turned to him and we kissed again.

I suddenly felt like we were being watched. I gently disengaged myself and looked over my companion's shoulder. My father stood their, a very disapproving look upon his face. I bristled. How dare he intrude! I had not asked him to keep an eye on me. I flung a nasty 'go away' look at him and relaxed back into the warm arms that held me. I felt safe there and welcome. There was a faint tickle of guilt trying to make itself felt in my consciousness. After all Gary *was* married. I pushed it determinedly away. This was only our first date and who knew what was going to happen? Later, when I looked, my father was gone.

For some time, I was too angry to call on my father. In fact, it was many months before I could bring myself to do so. In the meantime, my

6

relationship with Gary deepened. His marriage broke up and we became engaged.

Then one day I woke up and felt a huge hole in my happiness. The anger I had kept towards my father was gone. I missed him very much. So I called to him to come to me. At first nothing happened. I tried again and again and again. My heart started beating almost out of control, and it was very difficult to think clearly. It had been so long our bond was almost severed.

'Daddy, please come to me. I need to talk to you,' I called frantically.

I waited. A faint form tried to appear.

'Daddy, please come. I'm sorry. I love you.' It gradually grew more solid. I waited anxiously as the form wavered back and forth between the substantial and insubstantial.

'I love you, Daddy,' I repeated, and he was there.

I ran to him and wrapped my arms around him, tears streaming down my face. 'I'm sorry, Daddy. I'm sorry. I didn't mean to act so stupidly. I didn't mean to hurt you.'

He stroked my hair and kissed me on the forehead, like he used to do when he comforted me when I was a little girl. He brushed the tears away from my cheeks and smiled. 'Tell me what you've been up to.'

We spoke for hours. I told him all that I had done over the last several months. And he listened to me carefully. He smiled slowly and gathered me into his arms again.

I knew then that this was the last time I would see him.

'Daddy, what's wrong? What's going on?' I felt my heart quicken and my eyes opened wide with fear.

He pulled away so he could answer me properly. His eyes scanned my face as if he needed to remember every detail of what he was seeing.

'I have to go now, sweetie,' he said. He took my hands in his and kissed the back of each of them. 'I'm very proud of you. You know that, don't you?'

Practical Proofreading

I nodded. My heart hammered even louder.

'You know I came back because you needed me? Well, you don't need me anymore. You're strong and you're smart and you're beautiful.'

'NO, Dadddy!' I cried. 'No, you can't go. I won't let you.'

He gathered me to him again. 'You have to, sweetie. I just can't be here any more. It's not allowed. I have to rest now. I'm very tired.'

I looked at him then. I hadn't noticed before; he had always looked like he did in the photo Mum still kept on the mantelpiece. There were wrinkles round his eyes, now, and his hands were old and gnarled. My father had grown old and I hadn't noticed.

After a while he moved away, holding on only to my hands.

We held hands for as long as we could and then he was gone. He was satisfied I would be safe and happy.

And, I have been.

9

Even though my father no longer comes to me,
I know that ~~he~~ is with me.

Diary of a Sleep Apnoea Sufferer

Never have I felt so epxosed before, so naked, so utterly at the mercy of these torturers.

Sure, let's go have a sleep study! Sounds simple, doesn't it? No one tells you what it's really like though. Is this really worth the pain and humiliation for a sound night's sleep, some energy and no more snoring/

I guess it is.

At least, I'm not alone. Two other ladies and a man (who is keeping to himself) are sharing this experience with me. Well, not really sharing. More like they're just here, too. With the same problems I have, no doubt, or similar anyway.

God, I wish this night were over.
Had a little pause there. It was my turn to be wired. Then, kindly, they said I could go and watch television. One of the other ladies was done before me and the other is being done now. I don't know what I look like but the lady the across room looks

1

like some sort of weird alien or robot or something. She has half a dozen wires attached to her face, a couple on her neck and one in her hair. So do I. Not what you might call fashionable.

A couple of the areas where they've stuck electrodes are still stinging. I laughed when I saw the nurse pick up a tiny piece of sand paper. I didn't for long, though. I doubt I have any skin left on my face where she rubbed it, first with alcohol and then the sand paper. A deadly combination if ever I knew one.

Somehow I dont think I'd wish this torture on my worst, or best, enemy.

All three of us have been sitting here trying to watch television as if nothing is out of the ordinary. The man elected to stay in his room. I guess we intimidated him. Good for us!

Uh, oh, the nurse just popped in to see if any of us were ready to go to bed. Not yet, we all said, but I keep thinking that maybe I should get it over with. My courage is non-existent, however, so I'll sit

2

here for a little while longer.]

My bladder drove me out of the chair and to the toilet and so I decided to take the plunge. But so had everyone else, so I am waiting until someone is ready to plug me in.

 Well, here I am. All the wires from my head are plugged into the bed panel. I have a wire attached to each leg and they are attached as well to the bed. Then I have this bloody uncomfortable breathing thing stuck up each nostril. (The nurse said it was to measure the air coming out of my nose.) Finally, I have an oxygen monitor attached to a finger on my right hand.

How on earth am I supposed to sleep with all this garbage on? To top it all off, there is a video camera on the wall, staring straight at me. Great! No secrets for me anymore!

 Time to go to sleep, I guess.

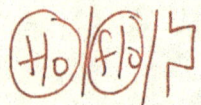 [I made it. It didn't take much to get to sleep,

although I can't say I slept normally. Every I time [ts] rolled over, I tangled all the wires and I was afraid I'd pull some out and then I'd have to come back and do it again. No way!

I only had to call the nurse once during the night, (although I was dead scared that I would have to get up and go to the loo, even though I don't normally)/ The tubes from my nose started to strangle my ears and I couldn't work out where they went to so I had to get the nurse to loosen them. I slept much better after that.

In the true form of nature and physics or whatever, it takes only a couple of minutes tops to remove all the wires from the various portions of my body.

I'm free! Hubby will here be in a few minutes [trs] so I better get dressed and pack my bag.

I probably did that in record time. My watch tells me I have time to go to the loo.

Hubby is here now. Come on, what are you

waiting for. You promised me a Maca's breakfast and even if that's out, I wanna get home.

Good-bye Austin Hospital. I hope to never see you again. At least not until I have the follow up sleep study once the official report comes back and my sleep apneoa is confirmed.

Ah, well, a good night's sleep probably is worth it!

Major 6 Page 75

It's Just Not Fair!

It's not fair, thought Sarah. It's just not fair! She was standing at the bus stop, waiting for the bus to Assumption College. It was the first day of Year 7. It meant a new school and being at the bottom of the ladder again.

The new school didn't worry her. Nor did being on the bottom of the ladder. But it wasn't fair that she had to go to a different school than all her friends.

'You'll meet new ones,' her mum had said, 'You wait, by the end of the first day you'll wonder why you were worried.'

She'd rolled her eyes, *Sure Mum, anything you say, Mum. But it's not you starting at a new school, it's not you being separated from your friends. It's just not fair!*

She grumpily kicked some innocent stones that were unaware of her mood or surely they would have found some way to out get of her way.

Other kids started to arrive. Kids, older,

wiser, more experienced in the way of school buses. When it finally arrived, she'd somehow ended up at the end of the queue, which wasn't fair seeing she had been the first there. She struggled up the steps with her bag. The crowded bus was full of happily chatting and, in some cases, singing kids from her age through to what looked like Year 12s. She stood at the top of the step, looking from an empty seat. The driver turned in his seat to help. After a few seconds, they both gave up. 'I'm sorry, love, but I think you'll have to stand. It's all right, thought, it's only about ten minutes to the college.'

'Thank,' she mumbled. Fat lot of good you are, she thought ungratefully.

'I'll make sure there's a seat for you tonight.' She smiled and moved down the aisle a little where there was space to stand between the bags.

Just as she settled, the bus lurched, and she nearly fell onto the bags at her feet. As it was they got a little trampled.

'Hey watch me bag. It's got me lunch in it,' a belligerent voice shouted at her.

She cr*n*iged. This was turning into her worst nightmare.

'Give over, Jack. Can't you see it's her first day and the poor kid has to stand and all. Why don't you offer her your lap? She's not bad looking, you know,' a slightly English voice defended her in a sniggering fashion.

Sarah felt the blood rush to her face and she looked at Jack only to find him considering her. The blood then proceeded to drain from her face.

'Leave her alone, guys. It hasn't been so long since you were one of the new kids. It's not fair to pick on her. Come here, I'll keep those two wolves from being nasty.' The girl who spoke was obviously someone with authority. Sarah didn't know whether Assumption had prefects or not like in Harry Potter, but if they didn't, this girl obviously had some

3

influence.

The guys started arguing and left her alone and so she moved down t where the older girl sat. There was more room on the floor there and so it was easier to stand.

'Hi, I'm Sarah McClean,' she said shyly, 'Thank you for that.'

'Oh, it's nothing. They always try to throw you new ones. Don't listen to them. They're not dangerous or anything, just stupid. I'm Joanne Carter. If you need anything just let me know, everyone knows me. Oh, meet Joy, she's my little sister. She starts today, too. Maybe you two will end up in the same class.'

They exchange 'Hi's' but both were feeling too daunted to chat.

It seemed like forever, but bus finally arrived at the school. With her new-found friends, Sarah fought her way off and managed to get out when she was meant to instead of being pushed to the back.

Joanne assured (everyone her) would sort *tr3* themselves out over the next couple of days and getting on or off would become much more orderly.

'The start of the year is always the worst. For everyone. Not only you newies. Just make sure you stick up for yourself and you'll be all right.'

np They headed into the school. Sarah thought it probably wasn't such a bad looking school but her heart still wanted to be with Nell at Whittlesea Secondary College.

anne Joyce noticed the downweed trend of her *ar* mouth. 'Come on, you'll be all right. There's about eighty new kids, all in the same boat as you. You'll make friends. You already know Joy. I'm sure you'll meet others.'

Sarah smiled at her gratefully but still felt like life was being terribly unfair. She had to admit that *Joanne* meeting ~~Joyce~~ and Joy was a stroke of luck,

5

though.

'Okay you two. I think you have to go to the auditorium where you'll be classed off and from there you'll enjoy a normal hard working day like the rest of us. I'll keep an eye out for you at recess. But remember, Joy, I'm only babying you today. Tomorrow you're on your own.'

'Okay, okay. I don't need "babying" today, though, so don't worry about it.' A glint of unshed tears gleamed in her eyes as she was afraid her big sister would take her up on her offer.

'No way. You know I promised Mum I'd look after you. Well, I am. For today. After that you should be right.'

The two new girls followed the directions and made their way to the auditorium

It seemed crowded but Sarah found herself already feeling a little more comfortable. The classes were divided, and Sarah and Joy found

6

Solutions to Exercises

 themselves sharing most of their subjects.

Sarah's grumpy mood was having a hard time lingering after this. And especially when she kept finding  familiar faces among the new flock. She, perhaps, couldn't put a name to them but the fish-out-of-water loneliness started to fade.

Of course, the last thing she would admit was that Mum was right!

But secondary school without her best friends looked like it might be all right after all.

She linked arms with Joy and headed off to their lockers. She was in secondary school now. None of that being led around by the hand. She had to organise herself and work hard. Maybe it wasn't fair that she had to go to a different school but maybe it was going to be okay, two.

Major 7 Page 91

Holiday Haunts to Die For

From The Spirits Travel Agency Inc.

I bet you've just died for a holiday. After your full haunting training you probably need something for your tired spirit. Here are the Top Five Holidays of Bad Luck for the haunting exhausted ghost.

first on our tour is the famous Death Valley, California, USA. The ghost towns have a social life that can't be beaten. The best spot in the valley is Ballarat named after an Australian goldmining camp. Catch up with some famous spooks and get some tips from the best. Accommodation is no problem once the living are scared off and then it's spiritual bliss for the weary.

MOving on to Tombstone, Arizona, will just turn your poltergeist inside out. Watch the re-enactment at the O.K. Corral / by the original participants. Be warned, keep your thoughts to yourself or you may find yourself in more than a re-enactment of one of the bloodiest episodes in the West. But maybe that's the excitement you are looking for. If you want a quieter time, be entertained by living as the local dead play their tricks.
The USA offers a plethora of other ghostly and magical places to visit. You might want to make a side trip before moving on with the rest of your tour. Let your agent know and I am sure you will have trouble deciding where to go.

Our next stop is the Dead Sea This is a bit of a jump from California to Israel, but, hey! We're not ghosts for nothing! The big attraction here is that even ghosts can float in the waters. The black mud baths should not be missed. They lift the most flagging of spirits. Situated 400 meters below sea level, it brings to life the heat of Satan's fires.

Another highly recommended vacation is a cruise on the Titanic. Bored of its Atlantic runs, it has been travelling between Europe and Australia for nearly half a century. It is a wonderful deep-sea experience featuring seaweed-shrouded cabins, rotting timbers and rusting hull.

Our stop final before returning to our respective haunts, is Queen Victoria Market, Melbourne, Australia. Unknown to most of the living this is one of the largest ex-cemeteries in the Southern Hemisphere. Many of the 10,000 souls buried here are experts in their haunting and use some of the most refined techniques ever employed. For those who wish an intellectual challenge this can be a real learning haunt.

I'm sure everyone will be able to find something interesting amongst these Five Top Ghostly Holidays, from phantasm to ghost. Costs are kept low with our tours as you use your own powers to travel. We look after all other details. So, with a little planning you need never have an unenjoyable holiday again. After all you'll be in this **afterlife** for a very long time.

Practical Proofreading

Main 8 Page 93

The Tale of Little Red Riding Hood

red stole from the sleeping house and disappeared into the dark city streets. She gathered her red coat close and buried her head in its hood. Her grandmother lived on the other side of the city.
She had been walking for quite some time when she ran into a strange man. He introduced himself as Mr Wilbur Wolfe and asked why she was out alone so late at night.
Red though tiny in stature, was as **bold** as they come. She straightened up and looked him in the eye. Her grandmother was ill and she was going to look after her. Little did he know that she was actually running away from home. Her parents had finally gone too far. They wouldnt let her do anything she knew her friends did.
Mr Wolfe bade her good night and be careful. He headed off down Union Street. Red continued down Main Street, where she loved to look in the shop windows and dream about buying everything she wanted.
Wolfe hurried and found Red's grand mother's house before Red had gone past her first store. He knocked and when grandmother answered, he adopted a high-pitched voice pretending to be Red needing to talk to her urgently.
Grandmother opened the door. Mr Wolfe pushed her inside, threatening her with a gunn in his pocket. He bound and gagged her and locked her in a cupboard. He put on some of Grandmother's clothes and makeup and

practiced her croaky voice. It wouldn't be Red looking after her grandmother tonight; he had plans to look after Red.

A little time passed, and he start to grow bored. Then a knock sounded on the front door.

"It's me, Grandma, called Red.

"Come in, dear. I'm in the lounge room," croaked Wolfe in his best grandmother voice.

Red thought her grandmother looked a little odd when she found her, but she was too upset with her own problems to wonder about her grandmother's looks.

"What is the matter, dear? It's very late for a visit, you know. Wolfe gestured for her to come closer and patted the seat beside him on the couch.

"It's horrible, Grandma/Mum and Dad won't let me do anything. It's so unfair. Can I come and live with you?"

"Well, that sounds like a good idea. I'm sure we could be very happy living together."

Red grew suspicious. She looked closer.

"Grandma, your ears are all hairy. I've never noticed that before."

"Well, dear, I'm taking a special tonic to give me energy and it's made the hair in my ears grow."

"Oh," said Red. "And your eyes look bigger and brown. I always thought you had blue eyes."

"That's my cataracts acting up. But they're all right."

"Grandma have you been working out/ Your arms

Practical Proofreading

look very muscly."

"Oh, yes, thank you, my dear. I have been exercising a little. It helps me with carting the firewood."

"And Grandma, your hands seem bigggger than they used to be. Are they all right?"

"Oh, yes dear. They need to be so I can hold onto you when you struggle."

Red realised she was trouble but knew what to do. They'd had classes on this at school. She jumped up.

Wolfe jumped up, too, and lunged at her. She dodged, stuck out her foot, and he fell flat on his face. She ran into the kitchen. She heard a banging coming from the pantry, as she grabbed the rolling pin down that her grandmother always had hanging by the stove, but Mr Wolfe was upon her. She swung around and hit him across the head as hard as she could. He swayed, dazed by the attack. She brought the rolling pin up into his groin. He screamed and fell to the floor in agony.

Red ran over to the pantry and let her grandmother out. Grandmother took the rolling pin while Red rang 000 for the police. Grandmother stood over Mr Wolfe. Every time he moved the rolling pin came down on a different part of his anatomy.

By the time the police arrived, Mr Wilbur Wolfe was more than happy to surrender himself to them. At his trial, he described Red and her Grandmother as 'demented' and 'in dire need of psychiatric help'. He was incarcerated for five years. When his time was almost up, he started a riot and received another three years for his efforts. He was a happy man

Major 9 Page 101

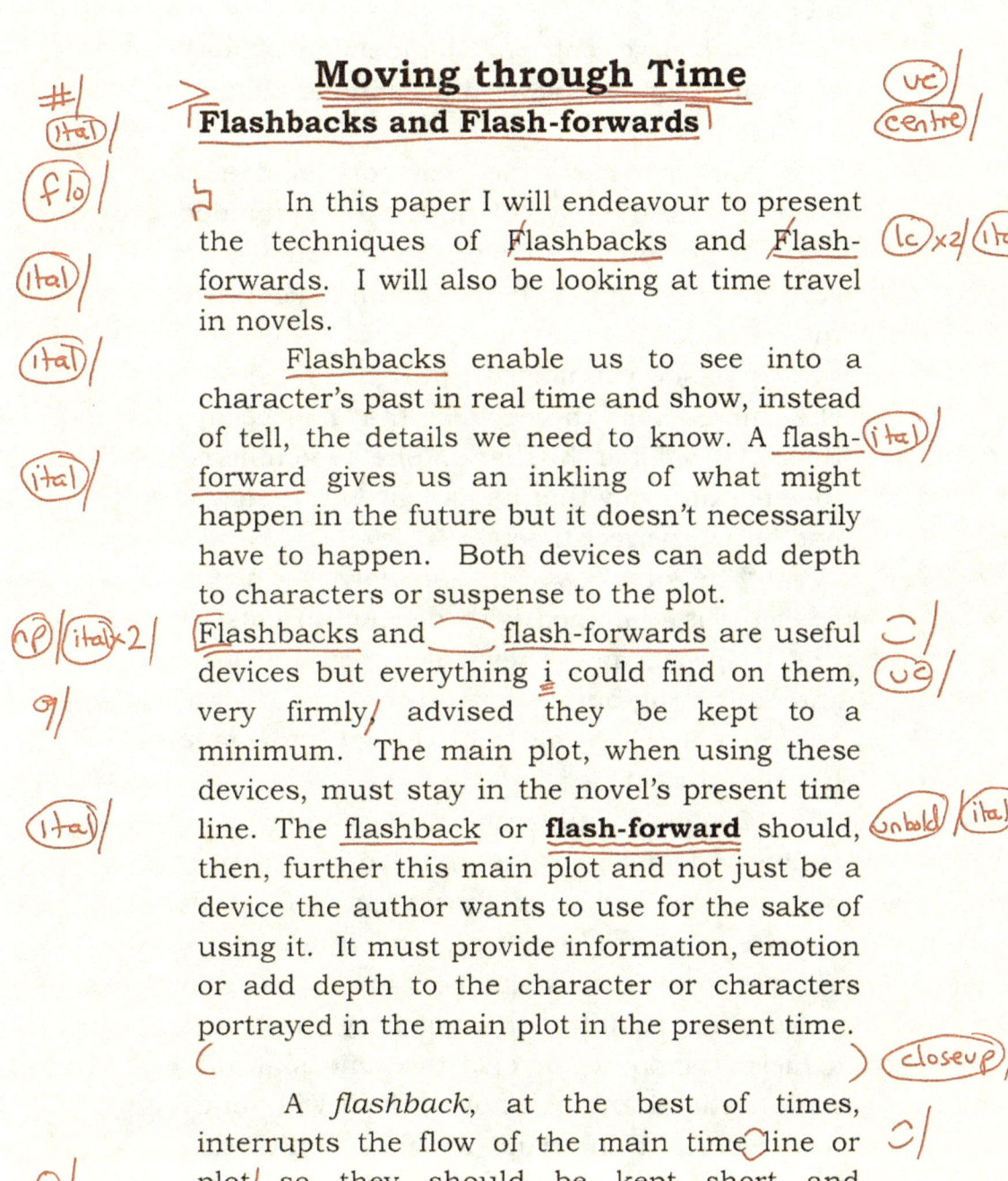

Practical Proofreading

memories.

Of course, entering the memory is fairly easy and there are several acceptable phrases to do this.

For example: "her memory suddenly went back to the day when…"; "this reminded him of the time…". There should then be a couple of uses of past perfect (had) to complete the transition.

"As she rummaged through the drawer, she came across the necklace that had been a present from her husband. She remembered the sparkling day that he had given it to her. It had been a perfect time.

"The sun was high and hot. The picnic basket was crammed with delicious treats. It was a special day. They both knew it. Daryl spread the rug out under the shade of a large oak far enough away from the lake to make the view perfect…

Continue your scene in real time using action and dialogue and then return to past perfect once or twice to show your reader that you are returning to the present. If necessary, another transition sentence can be used at this point. Exiting the memory must be achieved smoothly or else the time shift will appear stilted and will not work. It will annoy the reader and interrupt the flow of the story too much.

"Danielle had placed the necklace

around her neck so Daryl could admire it. But that wasn't possible anymore.

Amy ran into the room. She was winging that Jake was teasing her. Danielle replaced her treasured necklace. She would have to wait for another time to finish her reminiscences. "Okay, Amy, let's go see if we can sort this out." She took Amy by the hand and they went in search of Jake."

Flashbacks can also take place in a dream or a state of unconsciousness. However, the rules still apply / they must be necessary to the main plot in present time, they must be short, and they must be entered and exited smoothly. Dialogue can also be used to contain a *flashback* or flash-forward, as can the general narrative.

Flash-forwards are less common than *flashbacks*, it seems. I have written a story using a type of flash-forward, but I don't believe I have read any books with any in them. My story involved a young mother running away from her responsibilities. She boards a train and heads off to a new life. On the train she meets a man and they have a casual conversation. It turns out they are headed to the same town. When they arrive at the station, he gives her a lift and arranges some accommodation for her. She already has a job that she applyed for before leaving. Over the next several months,

3

the two become close and spend time together but no romantic attachments are formed. She talks to him often of the family she left behind. He feels she has made a mistake so arranges for her husband and children to come on a surprise visit. When she sees them, she knows she has been a fool.

At the next train stop, she jumps up and leaves, thanking her companion for his company. It's unclear in the story whether she fell asleep and dreamt about the possible future or whether there was some magical intervention by the other passenger. And that's the way I wanted it.

Flash-forwards are probably most often used with psychic episodes, where someone either has the ability to see into the future or has an episode of doing so. With so much new Age thinking around nowadays, this is an acceptable way of persuading the reader to suspend their disbelief.

Another form of flash-forward is the foreshadowing. It easy is to use and effective when ending a scene or chapter.

For example, "Sam wished he could rid himself of the sick feeling in his gut that told him something terrible was going to happen, and happen soon."

As can be seen, it acts as a hook to keep the reader interested, dangling something that might be in front of the readers eyes. It does not actually move the action into the future but in a way, moves the reader into the future, by having them wonder what is going to happen. It involves the reader and, therefore, is quite effective.

Various mechanisms such as the use of italics, a gap in the text, three asterisks are often used to shift the time frame, and make them more evident to the reader, thus helping to prevent any confusion as to what is happening.

A more sophisticated form of *flashback* is called the *time-shift*. It is more durable as a means to introduce a number of past experiences into the story. The types of phrases used to introduce the basic *flashback* are omitted.

To achieve this more subtle effect, you must concentrate on writing a seamless transition. This can be acheived by entering the consciousness of the POV character and by drawing the reader's attention away from the present scene with some generalisation, that causes the story to continue without being in a particular time. Then before the reader knows it, the story is taking place in a diffrent time.

There must a "novelistic present" where time occurs chronologically for *flashbacks* or *flash-forwards* to occur in any form. They must be able to exit and return to this time.

5

Flashbacks and *flash-forwards* should be avoided at times of high tension or critical stages in the story, as they will diffuse the excitement of the scenes.

Flashbacks are possibly most popular in romance and biographical novels, whereas *flash-forwards* are possibly used more in science fiction, and fantasy.

Before using the *flashback* and *flash-forward* techniques always consider whether the information needed can be, just as effectively, or more effectively, delivered through dialogue or a brief though. If a flashback or flash-forward is seen to be the best way to show what is needed, they must make sense and further the present plot and they should be kept short so the plot in the present does not become stale.

Where this is probably mostly true, if we take such works as H. G. Well's *Time Machine* when the time Traveller returns from his

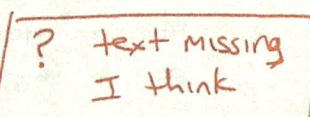
? text missing I think

Major 10 Page 119

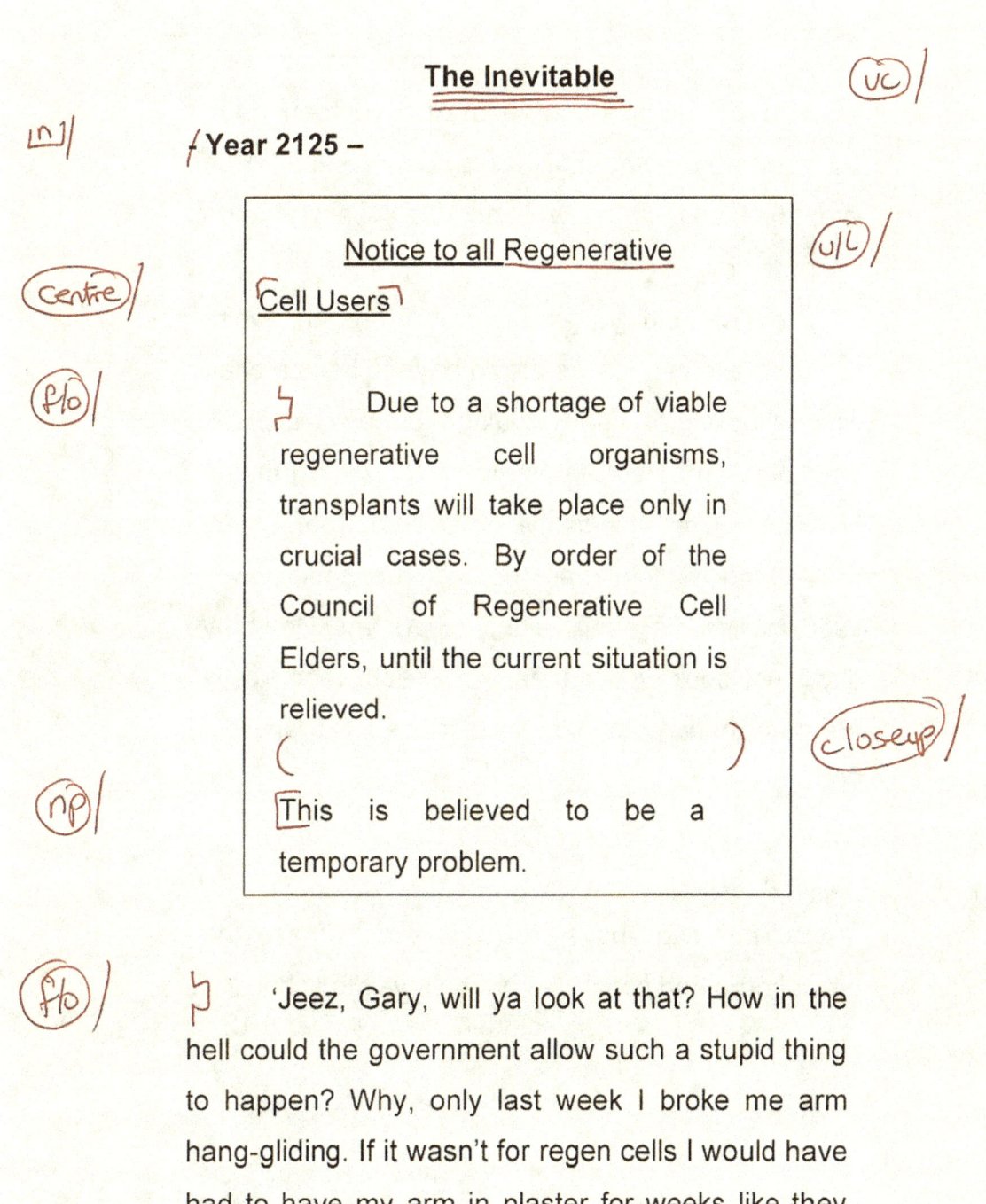

did in the old days. Bloody stupid, isn't it, Bob
looked round at his best friend. At seventeen years
old, they were both ambitious and opinionated, Bob
intent on becoming a lawyer and Gary wanting to do
bio-research.

'Yeah, did ya know that pre-regen, when
people broke their backs they'd have to be in a chair
with wheels 'cos they wouldn't be able to walk
anymore. I'm sure glad we live now. Jeez, I musta
broken me back at least five times now, Bob.

'And my old man, he told me people only
used to live for about eighty years av. Gee, my
dad's got socks older than that. Yeah, regen cells
are sure the way to live. I'm glad it's 2125 and not
2000.

The two boys moved away from the
noticeboard and continued on their way to school.

* * *

Year 2162

'Your Honour, Mister Gary Mansfield has been in a coma now for six months. Prior to his accident he showed promise of becoming one of this nation's most brilliant biochemists. At fifty-four years of age he is still a young man with a great deal to offer this society. I put to you the necessity to release regen cells to aid in his recovery.'

'Mr Davies, your arguments will be considered, and this court will reconvene tomorrow at ten a.m.'

Bob sat down. The hearing had been the toughest of his career. His best friend was dying and there was nothing they could do. Nothing except to administer the extremely rare regen cell treatment. He thought back thirty-five years earlier to when everyone used regen cells as if donning a new jumper.

No one had realised that by using regen cells so extensively there would become a shortage and they would almost revert to pre-regen cell times. It had been horrible watching rich people take advantage of the system and poor people die because they couldn't afford to do anything else.]

Then the authorities had introduced the hearings in order to assign the regen cells available in a more equitable way. At first it had seemed like an excellent solution but, law being law, clever, unscrupulous lawyers would drain their clients of all their funds and leave them stranded and in worse condition than when they started. The hearings started taking months. In the meantime, sufferers would die. As each case came forward it took longer and longer.

Rob prayed that the decision returned would be a favourable one.

He remembered the night of Gary's accident. Gary had rung him, sounding very excited about a breakthrough he had just made in his research. He had been on his way to show Bob his latest findings. It had piqued Bob's interest, for the first time in a long and jaded life. If Gary's accident had not occurred, all the misery and the hearings may not have been necessary, not only for Gary but for millions of others as well.

[Now they were at the final stage and all Bob

could do was cross his fingers.

* * *

Year 2220

'Hi, Gary, how's it goin'?' Bob felt thankful every time he heard Gary's voice.

'Not good, Bob. I'm glad you rang. I need your advice.' He went on to explain his dilemma.

'My God, man. They can't do that. First they develop regen cells and exploit them almost to extinction. Then once they've milked you dry in developing the artificial cell so there's plenty for everyone, they want you to develop a new strain. Who do they think they are? God? No, No, Gary. I can't just give you an answer over the phone. Come to my office, say in an hour? Okay, you see then.'

The line went dead.

Bob stood and went over to the window. The streets below were horribly crowded and even sixty floors up, through triple glazed windows, he could still hear the din of humanity below.

He picked up his binoculars and watched as a quarrel broke out amongst a couple of street vendors. They picked up their trolleys and rammed each other — once, twice. The third time both were thrown to the ground and their carts overturned. He could see mases of blood and was quite sure both were critically injured. In minutes an ambulance arrived and whisked them away. Bob knew that within the next hour or so both would be treated with regen cells to their damaged areas and with in days they would be back at their street stalls as if nothing had happened.

He saw this sort of thing all the time. No one respected life anymore.

He looked up the sky units being built. In the last fifty years every last inch of earth had been used. People now lived well into their second century and, in fact, it was believed, could almost live indefinitely.

Offshoots of regen cell technology had ensured an abundence of food for the ever-growing population.

He sighed and turned away from the depressing sight beyond his window. He knew what advice he he would give Gary when he arrived.

* * *

6

Year 2243 –

Bob turned up his radio.

"There have been a record number of deaths reported in the city in the past week. An increase of nearly two and a half thousand percent. From a normal five to six deaths, mostly from the common cold, to a staggering fifteen thousand recorded deaths. The cause of these deaths is still under investigation. More on the late news."

Gray had done the right thing. Bob had advised him to do as the government requested.

Bob looked across the coffee table at Gary. He looked old, all of his one hundred and ~~eighteen~~ thirty-five years showed in his face, as he listened to the rest of the news. Bob watched as a tear trembled at the corner of Gary's eyes and finally toppled over the rim to trickle slowly down his cheeks. Life was cruel. Life without death was more so.

THE CRYSTAL OF POWER

Dioptre looked around. Yesterday the village had been quiet. Now half the town was in panic, the other half in uproar. The Crystal of Power had been stolen during the darkest part of the night leaving the townspeople no longer under its protection, no longer encouraged to be trustworthy. Everyone knew who had perpetrated this unthinkable act. The Crystal must be returned to its tower, and returned quickly, or the whole country would be contaminated and evil would prevail. Dioptre hurried to her meeting with the king.

'Lady Dioptre, I request your aid in this quest. Your talents are great. You may be our only hope,' insisted the King.

'But, Your Majesty, surely your army would be more suited to pursuing the thief of the crystal? I am but a woman with a few tricks up my sleeve.'

'Your "tricks" are more powerful than my whole army. Gudren must be stopped and it will take

1

another witch to do it.'

Dioptre had her doubts that she alone could succeed, but she left the village that same afternoon on her griffin, Sepia.

'Come on, Sepia,' Dioptre urged, 'fly as if the wind would eat you if it caught you. We must reach Gudren's as quickly as we can.' They travelled quickly and far, making excellent time as the headed towards Gudren's keep.

On the edge of Gudren's domain the world tilted and Sepia fought to gain control as they plummeted. Gudren the evil witch, had shifted their dimension.

They plunged through the cloud cover and came to rest beside a road. They could hear singing coming out of a strange mist gathered before them.

Dioptre and Sepia felt bewildered by the magic worked on them and did not know what to make of the music.

Suddenly, a traveller stepped out of the mist.

'Do you require help, my Lady?' he inquired.

'Yes. Please tell me where we are?' said Dioptre, guardedly.

'Curious,' the traveller said under his breath. Out loud he said, 'You are in Acquitarius, my lady. I am *Prince* Myrrhdok, warlock, and your humble servant.' He bowed deeply. Her beauty enraptured him as it always enraptured those she met. This was one of her most useful powers.

'You are, perhaps, what is needed,' she mumbled. He looked at her questioningly. 'I am Dioptre, elf witch of Castella. I am on a quest demanding great urgency but I was caught in a trap and sent here. I must return immediately.'

'I will do all all in my power to help, my lady. Simply tell me what is needed and I will provide it.'

Both warlock and witch wore talismans to channel their powers. Each grasped hold of the other's talisman. dioptre spoke words of power. A portal formed before them, as she succeeded in breaking the strong spell that had sent them there.

'Thank you, my friend. My griffin and I must go now.' Dioptre and Sepia stepped through the portal. She gestured to close the gate, but at the last moment, Myrrhdok leapt through.

'You may need my help again, my lady,' he said and

3

strode off. For a moment Dioptre and Sepia stood and watched the strange warlock walk off into the distance and then they followed him.

They travelled swiftly and encountered no further traps, and arrived at the foot of Gudren's keep in no time. The evil witch's pet dragon, Petard, guarded the entrance. They could see the glow of the Crystal of Power high in the tower above.

'This dragon is a fierce one,' said Myrrhdok. 'If you can free the crystal, I will solve the problem of the dragon.' Dioptre nodded. With a small, graceful gesture Sepia and Dioptre vanished leaving only a faint breeze behind them.

Myrrhdok stepped out. He tossed an insubstantial ball of mist from one hand to the other, and whistled a cheery tune.

'Who goes there?' bellowed the ugly dragon.

'Only Myrrhdok, the magician, come to show you a trick.'

'Do not come closer.'

Myrrhdok stopped. He was close enough.

* * *

Practical Proofreading

Dioptre and Sepia flew swiftly to the top of the tower. There were no other guards there. Obviously, Gudren had ultimate faith in her dragon.

'Stay here,' she commanded Sepia and climbed off the griffin's back.

The tower surrounding the crystal shimmered with the evil being fed to the ball. Dioptre took down the crystal from its clawed stand. It felt heavy with evil. She fought the **suffocating** atmosphere as return to Sepia so they could fly to safety. Sepia tried to help her mistress to climb back onto her back, but she was badly feeling the effects of the evil. Dioptre, too, felt the effects of the evil seeping from the tower. She drew on the last of her power to weave a spell of clarity and protection around them. Then she flung herself upon Sepia's back and encouraged the griffin to lift into the air.

Sepia's wings beat more slowly each second they stayed on the tower. With an enormous effort she directed all the strength she could muster into lifting her wings and her body from the tower top. She hoped her strength would last long enough for them to reach safety beyond Gudren's reach. Sepia flew shakily away from the tower.

Gudren saw them flying away and knew immediately that her evil plan had failed. She screamed, enraged that they should be so bold. She flung bolts of lightning at them but Sepia was out of range.

Myrrhdok saw the griffin limping away and threw his mist at the dragon's eyes. It was not strong enough to kill it but it would confuse it. He turned and fled, as the evil witch began to scream.

the evil gradually seeped from the crystal as Dioptre and Sepia flew further and further away from Gudren's keep. When they deemed it safe, they landed to rest. Within minutes, Myrrhdok had joined them.

On the journey home, they exchanged stories of their relevant tasks. Dioptre amazed at Myrrhdok's courage in the face of an angry dragon.

Myrrhdok wondered what was to happen now. Dioptre was far too fascinating to leave behind and return to his own home. For now, though, he would just enjoy their journey back to Castella.

Gudren made one last attempt to resecure the crystal, when they were only a day away from the CRYSTAL Chamber. She ordered Petard to attack them. But Dioptre and Myrrhdok proved too strong. Together they summoned an earth spring and sent it into the air. The terrified Petard panicked and Gudren fell from its back, saving herself at the last moment by digging her claw-like nails into one of its wings. Petard turned and fled. He was not about to continue fighting when he knew he could not win. Dioptre, Myrrhdok and Sepia laughed at the sight of Gudren desperately clinging to the dragon's wing, screaming worse and worse obscenities at him, which he completely ignored. They were sure it would be quite some time before Gudren would be a problem again.

Two days had passed since the crystal was taken. There had been much destruction in that short time. Dioptre set the crystal in its rightful place in the Crystal Chamber. Almost immediately the people of Castella became the people she knew and loved again. The Crystal of Power was returned.

7

Major 12 Page 133

Sir Henry and the Dragon

Practical Proofreading

Chapter One

The two young knights fought valiantly, each a perfect match for the other. Wooden sword clashed on wooden sword. Henry blocked Tom, only to be blocked in turn. They fought back and forth, up and down the yard. Hours seemed to pass, but still they fought on, neither willing to give in to the other. Even when Henry's mum called them in for a drink and a snack, they kept on fighting, trying to outwit each other. But it was no good. They were to well matched. In the end they both collapsed on the grass, gasping for breath and exhausted, mutual in their agreement that their fight was a draw.

Henry closed his eyes against the sun still beaming strongly down onto them. His mind started to drift. He could hear Tom beside him, tapping his feet on the ground, could hear the birds calling in the trees as it grew closer to sundown and he could hear the creak of the clothesline as it turned lazily in the slight breeze.

A large shadow passed overhead. He could see it through his closed eyelids. He thought it must be a cloud. He hoped it wasn't going to rain. Then realised the sounds around him were different. There was no creaking clothesline. Instead there was the sound of wind whipping through trees. Tom's tapping feet changed into the sound of pounding hooves and the birdsong changed to enraged screams.

Henry opened his eyes and jumped to his feet. Coming straight for him was a blood red dragon. He grabbed the sword from the ground at his feet and dodged the sharp talons just in time.

Chapter 2

'Run, Sir Henry,' called a knight on the back of a huge armoured horse. Henry was still confused but all his instincts came to his rescue. The hours he had spent playing games on his computer meant that he had lightning quick reflexes and his mind was used to the extraordinary happening. When he had ~~Tome~~ he time would sit down and work out what on earth was going it on. But now he thought he had to find somewhere safe to hide.

Henry turned towards the forest and ran as fast as his armour-clad body could take him. He was, perhaps, not known for his speed, generally fear and need spurred him on faster than normal.

He knew from his computer games that zigzagging and mazes were wonderful diversions. He was still out in the open so zigzagging was the best thing for the moment but once inside the forest he would weave his way through the trees in a maze of a path that would make it difficult for the dragon to follow him.

As he ran, dodging first left and then right, forcing the dragon to continually shift its weight and swerve to follow him, Henry could hear the shouts of other knights around him. There were perhaps three or four others all trying to attract the dragon's attention away from Henry so he could escape but they were not having any success. The dragon was fixed on Henry and nothing was going to sway it from its

course.]
    Henry turned his head and took a quick look over his shoulder. The dragon was gaining on him. Henry waved his sword and shouted, 'You don't want to come near me. I'm good with this.' The next thing a bright yellow flame shot from the dragon's nostrils and Henry watched in dismay as his sword burst into flames. He dropped the flaming sword, turned and fled towards the forest.

Chapter 3

The dragon overtook him and landed just before the trees. He spread out his wings to prevent Henry from continuing. 'Your kind is not permitted here,' it bellowed. 'The forest belongs to the dragons.'

'Rubbish,' shouted Henry. 'The forest belongs to everyone. Anyway, the only reason we're here is because you are so nasty. Chasing us down and burning our swords and frightening everyone. That's why all these knights are hunting you, you know.'

'Go, or I will burn you up.' The dragon stared into Henry's eyes. Henry stared back. Suddenly Henry was not afraid. There was something else going on here.

'I don't believe you. You'll burn me as soon as I move.' Henry stepped cautiously to his right. The dragon followed, preventing him from going further. Spears shot past Henry. One pierced the right wing of the dragon and made him howl. Other spears followed. Henry turned and found an army bearing down on them. The three knights, who had been trying to distract the dragon before, streaked past, yelling for Henry to run. The dragon took to the skies again and Henry ran on into the safety of the forest.

He ran on and on until he was deep into the forest. Finally he had to stop to rest. He came upon a huge stack of tumbled boulders. When he searched for a safe place to sit he came across an opening to a cave. 'Just the thing,' he thought, and went through the opening. He stopped just inside to let his eyes get used to the dim light. It was enormous. He couldn't see the back of the cave at all and the sides were just dim shadows on the left and right of him. Henry moved in further. He tripped over something. It was a shield held in the tight grip of an armour-clad skeletalarm. He backed away from it, terrified at the gruesome sight. He moved further in and found more evidence of gruesome deeds. It began to occur to him that maybe the cave wasn't the safest place to be after all.

Chapter 4 ~~Four~~

¶ Henry kept wandering deeper into the cave. The light stayed at a soft dim glow and the temperature a warm summer's day warmth. It was odd; you would expect it to grow darker and colder the further you went into a cave. This was definitely not good!

Henry slowed his steps. He could sense something up ahead. It came up to about his waist level and was about his arms outstretched wide. As he drew closer he could see that there was a light cover over the top of the container. The container was rough and seemed to be made from branches and twigs and mosses. It looked a little like a nest. Carefully he lifted the cover and peeked underneath. Nestled in the centre of the nest were three orange eggs. 'Oh, no, this must be what he was worried about,' said Henry out loud.

'Yes and now you must die.' While Henry had been exploring (cave the) the dragon had crept in quietly behind him.

Chapter 5

Henry sprang around to face the huge creature. 'I will not harm your eggs,' said Henry trying to sound calm but in fact feeling like his legs were going to give way at any moment.

'You will not have the chance,' spoke the dragon carefully. The human language was not natural to the dragon. It was obviously an effort for him to form the words so Henry might understand. As it was, Henry had to listen carefully to hear the words between the growls and the hisses that came from the dragon's enormous mouth.

'I do not want to harm any humans,' said the dragon. 'I just want to be left in piece to raise my children. We are the last of our kind now. I will go away with my young once they are hatched and find a place where no man will walk. But I must be given tome for my eggs to hatch.'

'What happened to your wife,' asked Henry realising that it was normally the female dragon's duty to watch over the eggs.

A huge sorrowful sigh blew out from the dragon's nostrils. 'She was out hunting for food but the knights came and slaughtered her. Our eggs were only newly hatched but able to be left for short periods of tome. I have had to work hard to keep them alive since Medora was slain.'

'I should introduce myself,' said Henry. 'My

10

name is Henry.'

'I am Garanthal,' said the Dragon. 'You do not speak the way other humans speak. Why is that?'

'Um – actually if we are going to talk, would you mind lying down? My neck is getting sore.'

Garenthal was only too willing to oblige. There was something more here than met the eye. Garenthla wondered, even hoped, that he might find a solution to his problems.

Chapter Six

'I'm not really sure what happened, but I was playing at sword fighting with my friend, Tom. We were pretending to be knights, mighty knights, but neither of us could gain on advantage over the other. After playing for hours, at least, we agreed that the game was a draw. We lay down on the grass and I closed my eyes from the sun. The next thing I knew I was here, dressed like this and you were flying overhead. Dragons don't really exist where I come from, although we have lots of stories about them but no one has ever really seen one or found any remains either. Strange, hey?'

He looked up into the dragon's great face. Garenthal's fiery eyes were thoughtful and perhaps just a little confused.

'You say there are no dragons in your land?'

Henry nodded.

'And you don't know how you came to be here?'

Henry shoook his head this time.

'Well, Sir Henry, I think I might be able to return you to your tome and place. I didn't really want to kill you and as you won't be a threat once you go back I won't need to.

'I believe you may have passed through a doorway. There are a few in this land but not many know of them. I, however, know of one that you will be able to use. It is right here in this cave.'

12

'So ~~,~~ what do I have to do?' asked Henry, a little sad that he would have to leave this land of dragons, but he knew he needed to return.

'First, you need to think very strongly about your home. Have you got a strong image?' Henry nodded. He had closed his eyes to help him see it properly. The dragon moved closer and scooped up his eggs, depositing ~~him~~ [them] in a sack beneath his wing. 'Now wish with all your heart, that you were home and take a~~n~~ slow step forward.'

Chapter **Seven**

'Yeah, I think we should play something on the computer now. How about that new game Jason got for you? You know that one about dragons.' Tom shoved another piece of biscuit in his mouth.

Henry looked around. He was back home as if nothing had happened.

'What do you say?' Tom repeated.

'Yeah, okay.'

Henry heard a scratching sound outside the back window. He looked out to see a puff of smoke behind the carport. He was just about to yell fire when he spotted a huge eye winking at him through the gap.

'I'll be back in a minute, Tom. I left something outside. Go in and start up the computer.' He raced out the back door and up the yard.

'Garenthal, is that you? Is that really you?' he almost shouted.

'Ssh, Henry. Of course, it's me. Do you know any other dragons?'

'No, I mean, I thought it was all a dream or something. I didn't think you were real,' he whispered loudly.

'We are and thank you for the lift to your home land. Now we will be safe from hunters. As soon as it is dark we will leave and find a nice barren place that no one will find us in.' A little whimper sounded underneath Garenthal's wing.

'Is that …?' asked Henry.

14

'Yes, meet Dorian, Wildemere and Trance. They hatched as we passed through the portal.'

'I'll miss you, Garenthal,' said Henry. 'Can't you stay around so we can visit each other.'

'I'm afraid not, Henry. Your world is probably no safer than mine, especially as you say you have stories of dragons but no evidence. That probably means dragons were hunted to extinction many thousands of years ago. I need to keep my family safe and to do that I need to disappear.'

Henry nodded.

Tom suddenly called out the back door.

'I'll be right there, Tom,' Henry called back.

'I hope I'll see you again some tome,' said Henry.

'I hope so too,' said Garenthal. 'Perhaps when you're grown you'll remember me and come looking for my barren place. I'll make sure I leave markers. You'll understand them if you come looking.' Garenthal laid the tip of his wing on Henry's head. Henry felt a slight shock race through him that left him feeling warm. He knew that Garenthal had left him with the knowledge to find the dragons when the tome came.

He leant over and hugged the dragon as best he could, considering their hugely different sizes and then he gave him one last look and went inside to join Tom.

'What are you grinning about?' asked Tom.

15

'Oh, nothing. Nothing at all,' said Henry and not for the world would he ever tell anyone of his afternoon's adventure.

One last note

The marks I have used in this guide are those most commonly used in Australia.

If you Google 'proofreading marks' you will see some variations to these that are used in other parts of the world, although sometimes they are used in Australia, too.

If you become an in-house editor, then you will need to use whatever is commonly used by that organisation.

As a freelancer it's not so easy. I have often provided a summary sheet of the proofreading marks I use most commonly, so I know the layout designer and copy editor will understand exactly what I mean.

So long as you stick pretty close to the marks used in this guide and use the simplest change and write everything clearly, you should have no problems working towards other professionals.

Good luck in your future work!

About the Author

Pam Collings is an editor, proofreader and author with twenty years' experience in the publishing industry working as a proofreader, copy editor, manuscript assessor and tutor.

She has worked in educational publishing, and commercial publishing, as well as directly towards authors as both a proofreader and copy editor.

Pam has been fortunate enough to be a tutor for The Writing School and Australian College Qed where she tutored one of their proofreading and editing courses. She was also tutor for two writing courses for Australian College Qed where she was given the opportunity to write the proofreading course she tutored and contribute articles for several writing courses.

Pam has self-published two books of poetry – *Kaleidoscope* and *Mosaic*. Both are available through online bookstores including Amazon and Book Depository.

She is currently writing YA urban fantasy, which is a genre she very much enjoys reading, mainly for the spunk and resourcefulness of the characters that is generally portrayed and for the lightness of the writing.

Pam lives in Seymour, Victoria, Australia, with her two children and two cats. She enjoys painting when she can find the time and has developed a new love of gardening since COVID 19 hit. Spending time with friends and family and watching some good television or movies are among her top loves; the best being to devour a good book as often as she can find one.

Pam provides proofreading, copy editing and self-publishing services through her business, TB Books.

Contact: tbbooks@collings.id.au